TAKING CARE *of* BUSINESS

A ROADMAP FOR THOSE WHO WILL
SOME DAY TAKE CARE OF YOU

Phyllis W. McLaurin

Taking Care of Business
First Edition
ISBN: 978-0-578-66295-4
Copyright © 2019 Phyllis W. McLaurin, TCB 19 LLC
Copyright Registration #TX0008872119
Author: Phyllis W. McLaurin
Published by: TCB 19 LLC

Wholesale distribution is available. Contact publisher for pricing.

www.TCB19.com
TCB19LLC@gmail.com

CONTENTS

ACKNOWLEDGEMENTS

Writing this book has brought me tremendous joy as it helped remind me of the many clients I served over the years. While building lasting relationships, I learned so much about life from each of them.

Spending this time reflecting on life's lessons and how to prepare for the future has also caused me to realize how blessed I am in so many ways.

I had parents who raised me to be self-sufficient and strong in my faith. I am married to a loving and supportive husband. Blessed with children and family whom I love and cherish, in addition to supportive friends who are very dear to me. I thank each and every one of them for their love and friendship.

To the many co-workers, mentors, and colleagues that helped me grow in my career and personal life, I appreciate you more than you know.

And with tremendous gratitude, I thank God for the path he has allowed me to travel, for his everlasting gift of love, guidance and joy.

Phyllis W. McLaurin

INTRODUCTION

It was November 2, 2013 and my husband and I were traveling home from North Carolina. I had spent the last four months helping take care of my mother before she passed away. My husband was very quiet while driving . . . I assumed to allow me to grieve silently and to process what lie ahead. As the oldest child in our family, I assumed the responsibility for settling her affairs yet that was going to be a challenge with me living out of state. Thankfully my brother still lives in our hometown and was a tremendous help in orchestrating tasks locally on our behalf. I had recently retired after 42 years in banking, so I guess I was deemed to be the most knowledgeable of the steps necessary to see this through. As a financial advisor, I had helped guide many clients over the years and witnessed lots of heartache and resentment due to poor planning.

Thankfully, I had been given the opportunity to gather information from Mother before her death. I thought about how thankful I was to be aware of her wishes and to know the details concerning her will, assets, insurance info, etc. That's when it occurred to me that other than creating our wills, my husband and I had done little to plan for the day that we could no longer handle OUR affairs. All of our children lived out of state and didn't even possess a key to our home, much less know anything about our possessions, health related issues, finances or how we ran our daily lives. The more I thought about the process of settling Mother's affairs, the more worried I became about our own! What would happen if we were both in a car accident as we traveled home . . . our children wouldn't know where to begin, much less know our wishes for the end of our lives! So, I reached into my briefcase and pulled out a pen and tablet and began to make notes.

Needless to say, this task wasn't completed in an hour. Years later I am still adding to the list as I write this guidebook. I have shared my story with family and friends and conducted many sessions helping others understand and appreciate the importance of addressing this critical issue. The benefits of creating a roadmap for those that you trust to take care of you and/or your affairs.

While I have years of financial experience, I am not an attorney, therefore I frequently note in this roadmap when you should seek legal advice. Much of this information is based on experience and good common sense. As I mentioned earlier, I have witnessed many family conflicts and unnecessary hardship due to a lack of planning and appropriate sharing ahead of time. I hope that you find this information useful and that it motivates YOU to TAKE CARE OF BUSINESS. Trust me when I say it will be one of the greatest gifts you can give your loved ones.

I have chosen to provide the suggested list of information in bullet point formatting as most of it is self-explanatory. I've also included some blank space in the workbook of each chapter to remind you to jot down anything pertinent to YOUR particular situation that I may not have included.

The checklists are separated by category such that your loved one or caregiver can quickly find the information they might be looking for.

Depending on your individual circumstances, you may need to create separate checklist documents (for every chapter) for each spouse or partner. In most chapters however, one document indicating which individual the information belongs to is sufficient.

Note at the end of **Chapter 1: Personal Profile,** I HAVE chosen to include two profile documents in order to clearly specify each individual's information.

The checklist documents for the remaining chapters will ask for specific titles and ownership which should be sufficient for future reference. It is also a good idea to make copies of important documents to place in your *individual* Taking Care of Business **TCB Folder.** I will suggest what to include in this folder throughout this Roadmap. I will also discuss later some options for securing, sharing and storing the informational document that you are about to create.

Important Note: Your information should be reviewed and updated at least annually. I recommend this be done each year when you complete your taxes. If significant changes occur during the year, the information should be updated as soon as possible.

HOW TO BEST NAVIGATE
THE ROADMAP

- Answer questions that pertain to your circumstances.

- Tips will be provided to help you think through what's important.

- In some cases, the check list is more thorough than the text, so follow the checklist carefully.

- Prompts you to make copies of important documents to place in your **TCB Folder.**

- Following the chapter subject matter helps you create a final "Informational" document for your **TCB Folder.**

- Consider if you need to create just one document, or a separate one for your spouse/partner.

- As you read through the text, space is provided to make notes to yourself, but it is best to state the exact information you are trying to convey via the checklists at the end of each chapter.

- It's OKAY to scratch out and mark up this book . . . this is your working document.

- Be sure to indicate the date (beside each subtitle) that you are recording that specific information.

- Extra pages are provided at the end of each chapter for changes/additions in the future. Be sure to indicate the date of new information.

- You may want to consider creating a "Word Document" of only the information that pertains to you and your household after you've read through this roadmap. It will make it easier to update. I recommend you still categorize as suggested for easier reference.

Note: The information you will be recording in this document should **NOT** be considered a substitution for an official will or estate plan created via the laws of the state you live in. Remember, this is simply a roadmap to inform your loved ones of the necessary information needed to care for you when the time comes and guidance on where to find **YOUR** legal documents, necessary to settle your affairs someday.

SUGGESTIONS FOR CREATING YOUR TCB FOLDER

Purchase several multi divided folders and label each divider or create separate folders and place in large accordion file folders. Listed are suggested labels that could be applicable to you:

- Birth, Death, Adoption, Citizenship and Marriage Certificates
- Copies of Driver's License and Passport
- Motor Vehicle Titles
- Home, Car, Boat, etc. Insurance Documents
- Health Related Insurance Documents
- Life Insurance Documents
- Passwords for Access
- Military Records
- Divorce Papers
- Will, Power of Attorney, and/or Trust Documents
- Other Legal Documents
- Ownership of Burial Plot, Columbarium, etc.
- Pet Registrations
- Certificates of Recognition, etc.
- Real Estate Deeds
- Miscellaneous Property Documentation
- Note Receivable (signed copy) that you are owed or that you owe someone else.
- Loan Documents
- Appraisals, Receipts, and Pictures of Art, Jewelry, Antiques
- Appraisals Coin, Stamp, and other Collections
- Copyrights, Patents, and Royalties
- Contracts (copies)
- Business Related Documents
- Ancestry Documentation
- Gun Information and/or Registrations
- Service Providers
- Medical Information/Documents
- Tax Information
- Burial/Funeral Insurance and Other Plan Documents

CHAPTER 1

Let's Start at the Beginning
Your Personal Profile

Every individual's situation is different . . . you are either single, married, in a relationship, divorced, remarried or widowed. You have children, don't have children, or need to rely on a trusted relative or friend when the time comes to care for you or to manage your affairs. You shouldn't assume WHAT they might already know or remember, so plan to document everything. Below is a suggestion of where to begin and information you need to start gathering for both you and your spouse:

- 📁 **Full, Legal Names** – you and your spouse or partner.

- 📁 **Birthdates** – in addition, note the County (or Parish) and State of births

- 📁 **Social Security Numbers**

- 📁 **Home Address** – it is also a good idea to list any previous home addresses which can be very beneficial in settling estates and recovering unclaimed property.

- 📁 **Mailing Address** – if different from home address. If address is a post office box, indicate location of the post office.

- 📁 **Phone Numbers** – home, cell, and business (if applicable) On your cell phone, consider adding the letters ICE (**I**n **C**ase of **E**mergency) beside the name of your spouse or someone that should be contacted in case of an emergency should you not be able to communicate such.

- 📁 **Fax Numbers**

- 📁 **Email Addresses**

- 📁 **Children's Contact Information** – especially if they are no longer living at home. Include their full names, addresses, birthdates, and date of death if any are deceased. This information is sometimes necessary when settling an estate.

- 📁 **Full Name of Parents and Siblings** – this information may come in handy in the future for a number of reasons.

- 📁 **Information on Spouse/Partner's Family Members** – parents, siblings and children, especially if you are remarried. You never know when you (or your child) may have to get involved in settling the estate of a spouse/partner who owns separate property or shares partial interest with individuals not familiar to you or your immediate family.

- 📁 **Information on Former Spouse(s)** – name and how marriage was dissolved (death or divorce)

- 📁 **Designated Guardian of Your Children** – should something happen to you while they are still minors. Also necessary if you have a special needs child. This should also be included as part of your will.

- 📁 **Important Contacts** – list the names of individuals (along with their contact information) that are familiar with you, your business or assets, and can assist family members as needed. *Note:* there is further discussion below and in the following Chapters concerning business partners, professional advisors, etc.

- 📁 **Driver's License Numbers** – for identification purposes. Also, the driver's license should be canceled at death to protect from identity theft. I also suggest putting a copy of each person's driver's license in the **TCB Folder**.

- 📁 **Passport Numbers** – include a photocopy of all passports in the **TCB Folder**.

- 📁 **License Plate Numbers** – for any vehicles owned and driven. I had a close friend whose father was in the beginning stages of Alzheimer disease and wandered far from home one morning in his car. He was found later in the day because his daughter knew his license plate number and was able to provide that to the police.

- 📁 **Passwords: Computers, Online Accounts, Cell Phones** – Also note passwords of any specific digital documents located in your computer files or online drives.

- 📁 **Faith Information** – list your denomination, church you attend or are a member of, and the pastor's name, and contact information. Your family members will then know who to contact if you become ill, hospitalized or pass away.

- 📁 **Personal Attorneys** – list the names of your attorneys and their contact information. You should indicate which legal documents or other contracts each attorney may have prepared on your behalf.

- 📁 **Personal CPA** – list the name of your CPA and their contact information. Again, indicate which services this professional routinely provides for you.

📁 **Pets** – list the name of the Veterinarian that you use for your pets as well as any medications, allergies, conditions, etc. your pet may have. Information that someone would need to know if they provided temporary care. Also indicate if you typically board your pet and information concerning that service. Finally, indicate your wishes for ongoing care/ownership of any pets you may leave behind.

📁 **Military Records**

✎ **Other Important Facts Relative to you**

Note to self: _____

_____

_____

_____

You may assume that your loved ones know all the important information that you are in the process of recording here, but that is not always the case. Hopefully, you are beginning to realize the importance of doing this NOW!

Now that you have gathered personal information let's start documenting it for your **TCB Folder.**

ROADMAP
Personal Profiles

First Person Profile

Full Legal Name _____

Date of Birth ___ / ___ / _____ County/Parish _____

City _____ State _____ Country _____

Social Security # _____

Current Home Address _____

How long have you lived at this address? _____ years

Former Home Addresses: _____

_____

_____

Current Mailing Address (P.O. Box if applicable) _____

_____

Home Phone # _____

Cell Phone # _____ Cell Phone Passcode _____

Business Phone # _____ Fax # _____

Email Address _____ Password _____

Email Address _____ Password _____

Email Address _____ Password _____

Driver's License # _____ State of Issue _____

Issue Date ___ / ___ / _____ Expiration Date ___ / ___ / _____

Passport # _____ State/Country of Issue _____

Issue Date ___ / ___ / _____   Expiration Date ___ / ___ / _____

Occupation _____

Employer and Address _____

_____

Are you Retired?   ☐ Yes   ☐ No   *If yes,* Date of Retirement ___ / ___ / _____

Military Veteran   ☐ Yes   ☐ No   *If yes,* Branch of Service _____

Serial # (DD214) _____

Educational Background/Degrees

_____

_____

_____

Marital Status   ☐ Single   ☐ Married   ☐ Divorced   ☐ Widowed

Spouses' Full Legal Name _____

Note: Their information should be fully documented in the following Second Person Profile.

Former Spouse's Information

1. Full Legal Name _____

Date of Birth ___ / ___ / _____   Date of Divorce ___ / ___ / _____

Date of Death ___ / ___ / _____

2. Full Legal Name _____

Date of Birth ___ / ___ / _____   Date of Divorce ___ / ___ / _____

Date of Death ___ / ___ / _____

Children's Information

First Child

Full Legal Name _____ Date of Birth ___ / ___ / _____

Current Address _____

Phone # _____ Email Address _____

Spouse's Full Legal Name _____

Their Children's Full Legal Names

1. _____ Date of Birth ___ / ___ / _____

2. _____ Date of Birth ___ / ___ / _____

3. _____ Date of Birth ___ / ___ / _____

4. _____ Date of Birth ___ / ___ / _____

Other important information concerning this particular child and their family, including date of death if they have passed away.

_____

_____

_____

Second Child

Full Legal Name _____ Date of Birth ___ / ___ / _____

Current Address _____

Phone # _____ Email Address _____

Spouse's Full Legal Name _____

Their Children's Full Legal Names

1. _____ Date of Birth ___ / ___ / _____

2. _____ Date of Birth ___ / ___ / _____

3. _____ Date of Birth ___ / ___ / _____

4. _____ Date of Birth ___ / ___ / _____

Other important information concerning this particular child and their family, including date of death if they have passed away.

_____

_____

_____

Third Child

Full Legal Name _____ Date of Birth ___ /___ /_____

Current Address _____

Phone # _____ Email Address _____

Spouse's Full Legal Name _____

Their Children's Full Legal Names

1. _____ Date of Birth ___ /___ /_____

2. _____ Date of Birth ___ /___ /_____

3. _____ Date of Birth ___ /___ /_____

4. _____ Date of Birth ___ /___ /_____

Other important information concerning this particular child and their family, including date of death if they have passed away.

_____

_____

_____

Fourth Child

Full Legal Name _____ Date of Birth ___ /___ /_____

Current Address _____

Phone # _____ Email Address _____

Spouse's Full Legal Name _____

Their Children's Full Legal Names

1. _____ Date of Birth ___ /___ /_____

2. _____ Date of Birth ___ /___ /_____

3. _____ Date of Birth ___ /___ /_____

4. _____ Date of Birth ___ /___ /_____

Other important information concerning this particular child and their family, including date of death if they have passed away.

_____

_____

_____

Please check here ☐ if you have additional children and are providing their information in the blank pages and placing it in your **TCB Folder**.

Note: I suggest listing step children if they are relevant to your long-term care, business, or part of your estate plan.

Children's Guardian: Note here the name and information of the individual that you have named as guardian for any underage or special needs child per instructions of your WILL.

Name _____ Relationship _____

Address _____

Phone # _____ Email Address _____

Information Concerning My Parents

Father's Full Legal Name _____

Address _____ Phone #_____

Date of Birth ___ /___ /_____ Date of Death ___ /___ /_____

Place of Burial _____

Mother's Full Legal Name _____

Address _____ Phone #_____

Date of Birth ___ / ___ / _____ Date of Death ___ / ___ / _____

Place of Burial _____

Information Concerning My Siblings

1. Name _____ Phone # _____

Address _____

2. Name _____ Phone # _____

Address _____

3. Name _____ Phone # _____

Address _____

4. Name _____ Phone # _____

Address _____

Please check here ☐ if you have additional siblings and are providing their information in the blank pages and placing it in your **TCB Folder**.

Note: If any siblings are deceased, note that information along with date of death.

Computer Information

Username/Password for Computer(s)

Desktop Username _____ Password _____

Laptop Username _____ Password _____

List documents on computer that are password protected. Note which software you used to create the documents.

1. Document File Name _____

Password _____ Program _____

2. Document File Name _____

Password _____ Program _____

3. Document File Name _____

Password _____ Program _____

4. Document File Name _____

Password _____ Program _____

Note: You will have the opportunity to provide password information on bank and investment accounts later.

Religious Information

Faith Denomination _____

Church I Regularly Attend/Member of _____

Address of Church _____ Phone # _____

Pastor's Name _____ Phone # _____

Pets

1. Name _____ Breed _____ Age _____

Allergies/Conditions _____

Medications _____

Need to know habits/issues _____

_____

_____

2. Name _____ Breed _____ Age _____

Allergies/Conditions _____

Medications _____

Need to know habits/issues _____

_____

_____

3. Name _____ Breed _____ Age _____

Allergies/Conditions _____

Medications _____

Need to know habits/issues _____

_____

_____

Veterinarian

Name _____

Address _____

Phone # _____ Email Address _____

Pet Care Facility or Home Care Provider _____

Address _____

Phone # _____ Email Address _____

Wishes for ongoing care or ownership of your pets _____

_____

_____
                                                        ,
_____

Contacts

Personal Attorney _____

Address _____

Phone # _____ Email Address _____

List of legal documents or contracts prepared:

1. Document Title _____

Date ___ / ___ / _____ Location of Original _____

2. Document Title _____

Date ___ / ___ / _____ Location of Original _____

3. Document Title _____

Date ___ / ___ / _____ Location of Original _____

4. Document Title _____

Date ___ / ___ / _____ Location of Original _____

Personal CPA _____

Address _____

Phone # _____ Email Address _____

Services this individual provides:

_____

_____

_____

Awards and/or Recognitions During My Lifetime:

_____

_____

_____

_____

_____

_____

Other Important Information to Document or Share:

_____

_____

_____

_____

_____

_____

Second Person Profile

Note: It may or may not be necessary to complete duplicate information already in First Person Profile.

Full Legal Name _____

Date of Birth ___ / ___ / _____ County/Parish _____

City _____ State _____ Country _____

Social Security # _____

Current Home Address _____

How long have you lived at this address? _____ years

Former Home Addresses: _____

_____

_____

Current Mailing Address (P.O. Box if applicable) _____

_____

Home Phone # _____

Cell Phone # _____ Cell Phone Passcode _____

Business Phone # _____ Fax # _____

Email Address _____ Password _____

Email Address _____ Password _____

Email Address _____ Password _____

Driver's License # _____ State of Issue _____

Issue Date ___ / ___ / _____ Expiration Date ___ / ___ / _____

Passport # _____ State/Country of Issue _____

Issue Date ___ / ___ / _____ Expiration Date ___ / ___ / _____

Occupation _____

Employer and Address _____

_____

Are you Retired? ☐ Yes ☐ No *If yes,* Date of Retirement ___ / ___ / _____

Military Veteran ☐ Yes ☐ No *If yes,* Branch of Service _____

Serial # (DD214) _____

Educational Background/Degrees

_____

_____

_____

Marital Status ☐ Single ☐ Married ☐ Divorced ☐ Widowed

Spouses Full Legal Name _____

Former Spouse's Information

1. Full Legal Name _____

Date of Birth ___ / ___ / _____   Date of Divorce ___ / ___ / _____

Date of Death ___ / ___ / _____

2. Full Legal Name _____

Date of Birth ___ / ___ / _____   Date of Divorce ___ / ___ / _____

Date of Death ___ / ___ / _____

Children's Information

Note: Add if different than previously recorded.

First Child

Full Legal Name _____ Date of Birth ___ / ___ / _____

Current Address _____

Phone # _____ Email Address _____

Spouse's Full Legal Name _____

Their Children's Full Legal Names

1. _____ Date of Birth ___ / ___ / _____

2. _____ Date of Birth ___ / ___ / _____

3. _____ Date of Birth ___ / ___ / _____

4. _____ Date of Birth ___ / ___ / _____

Other important information concerning this particular child and their family, including date of death if they have passed away.

_____

_____

_____

Second Child

Full Legal Name _____ Date of Birth ___ / ___ / _____

Current Address _____

Phone # _____ Email Address _____

Spouse's Full Legal Name _____

Their Children's Full Legal Names

1. _____ Date of Birth ___ / ___ / _____

2. _____ Date of Birth ___ / ___ / _____

3. _____ Date of Birth ___ / ___ / _____

4. _____ Date of Birth ___ / ___ / _____

Other important information concerning this particular child and their family, including date of death if they have passed away.

_____

_____

_____

Third Child

Full Legal Name _____ Date of Birth ___ / ___ / _____

Current Address _____

Phone # _____ Email Address _____

Spouse's Full Legal Name _____

Their Children's Full Legal Names

1. _____ Date of Birth ___ / ___ / _____

2. _____ Date of Birth ___ / ___ / _____

3. _____ Date of Birth ___ / ___ / _____

4. _____ Date of Birth ___ / ___ / _____

Other important information concerning this particular child and their family, including date of death if they have passed away.

_____

_____

_____

Fourth Child

Full Legal Name _____ Date of Birth ___ / ___ / _____

Current Address _____

Phone # _____ Email Address _____

Spouse's Full Legal Name _____

Their Children's Full Legal Names

1. _____ Date of Birth ___ / ___ / _____

2. _____ Date of Birth ___ / ___ / _____

3. _____ Date of Birth ___ / ___ / _____

4. _____ Date of Birth ___ / ___ / _____

Other important information concerning this particular child and their family, including date of death if they have passed away.

_____

_____

_____

Please check here ☐ if you have additional children and are providing their information in the blank pages and placing it in your **TCB Folder.**

Note: I suggest listing step children if they are relevant to your long-term care, business, or part of your estate plan.

Children's Guardian: Note here the name and information of the individual that you have named as guardian for any underage or special needs child per instructions of your WILL.

Name _____ Relationship _____

Address _____

Phone # _____ Email Address _____

Information Concerning My Parents

Father's Full Legal Name _____

Address _____ Phone #_____

Date of Birth ___ / ___ / _____ Date of Death ___ / ___ / _____

Place of Burial _____

Mother's Full Legal Name _____

Address _____ Phone #_____

Date of Birth ___ / ___ / _____ Date of Death ___ / ___ / _____

Place of Burial _____

Information Concerning My Siblings

1. Name _____ Phone # _____

Address _____

2. Name _____ Phone # _____

Address _____

3. Name _____ Phone # _____

Address _____

4. Name _____ Phone # _____

Address _____

Please check here ☐ if you have additional siblings and are providing their information in the blank pages and placing it in your **TCB Folder.**

Note: If any siblings are deceased, note that information along with date of death.

Computer Information

Username/Password for Computer(s)

Desktop Username _____ Password _____

Laptop Username _____ Password _____

List documents on computer that are password protected. Note which software you used to create the documents.

1. Document File Name _____

Password _____ Program _____

2. Document File Name _____

Password _____ Program _____

3. Document File Name _____

Password _____ Program _____

4. Document File Name _____

Password _____ Program _____

Note: You will have the opportunity to provide password information on bank and investment accounts later.

Religious Information

Faith Denomination _____

Church I Regularly Attend/Member of _____

Address of Church _____ Phone # _____

Pastor's Name _____ Phone # _____

Pets

1. Name _____ Breed _____ Age _____

Allergies/Conditions _____

Medications _____

Need to know habits/issues _____

_____

_____

2. Name _____ Breed _____ Age _____

Allergies/Conditions _____

Medications _____

Need to know habits/issues _____

_____

_____

3. Name _____ Breed _____ Age _____

Allergies/Conditions _____

Medications _____

Need to know habits/issues _____

_____

Veterinarian

Name _____

Address _____

Phone # _____ Email Address _____

Pet Care Facility or Home Care Provider _____

Address _____

Phone # _____ Email Address _____

Wishes for ongoing care or ownership of your pets _____

_____

_____

_____

Contacts

Personal Attorney _____

Address _____

Phone # _____ Email Address _____

List of legal documents or contracts prepared:

1. Document Title _____

Date ___ / ___ / _____ Location of Original _____

2. Document Title _____

Date ___ / ___ / _____ Location of Original _____

3. Document Title _____

Date ___ / ___ / _____ Location of Original _____

4. Document Title _____

Date ___ / ___ / _____ Location of Original _____

Personal CPA _____

Address _____

Phone # _____ Email Address _____

Services this individual provides:

_____

_____

_____

Awards and/or Recognitions During My Lifetime:

_____

_____

_____

_____

_____

_____

_____

Other Important Information to Document or Share:

_____

_____

_____

_____

_____

_____

_____

Changes and Additional Information (remember to date)

Changes and Additional Information (remember to date)

CHAPTER 2

Personal Real Estate and Other Assets

So, yes . . . your children, family or partner know where you currently live and the address, but do they know if you have an outstanding mortgage balance on your home?

Do They Know . . .

☐ about any other real estate you might own or have an interest in?

☐ the identity, value and location of your other assets?

☐ about debt that may be owed to you or business interest or valuable collections?

Following is a suggested list which doesn't include liquid assets such as bank, investment or retirement accounts. These will be noted and discussed in **Chapter 3: Financial**.

🖋 **Improved Properties or Vacant Land** – list the addresses of any properties, **as well as the legal description**, including your home (if owned).

It is extremely important to note if any of these listed properties are owned jointly and if so, the full names of all owners (ex: siblings or other family members and/or friends/ business partners).

If married, indicate if the property is considered a **community asset** or **separate property** and note the full names of the property ownership as held in public records.

If you have multiple real estate or vacant land, you will want to list them separately. If some are rental, be sure to note who manages those properties if someone other than you. Indicate how the title is held, ie. individually, joint tenancy (except in Louisiana) or in a corporate/partnership/LLC name. Also note where each property is located (parish or county/state) and when the original sale (or transfer to you) took place.

You will be given the opportunity in **Chapter 3: Financial** to note any mortgages or debt outstanding on any real estate. However, if the property/properties are debt free, I recommend noting this and placing copies of the individual deed, which includes the legal description, in your **TCB Folder** with other important documents. Don't forget to indicate if any of the properties have periodic assessments such as homeowner dues.

🖋 **Shared Properties** – list Time Shares or any property owned with other individuals. *Note*: any annual dues that may be assessed.

- 🖊 **Commercial or Business Real Estate** – list in this category if owned personally. If, however the property ownership is part of your business, document along with other information as suggested in **Chapter 6: Business Information** which outlines all your business assets and information.

- 🖊 **Offsite Storage** – location of any offsite storage along with any combination or security codes necessary to enter the site. Also note the location of keys necessary to unlock the storage unit. Include location of offsite storage or rental spaces for boats, campers, motor homes, etc.

  Consider placing a list of any important/valuable items (and their value) that are in the storage unit in your **TCB Folder.**

Note to self: _____

_____

_____

_____

- 🖊 **Vehicles** – provide details of the make and model of cars, motorcycles, boats, campers and other licensed assets that you own. Note where titles are kept if they are debt free. If financing is outstanding, list the details of any car/vehicle loans as suggested in **Chapter 3: Financial.** Be sure to always include account/loan numbers.

- 🗁 **Business Assets** – See **Chapter 6: Business Information**

- 🖊 **Oil, Timber, Gas and Mineral Interest** – you will be prompted to include details on the land agent, if any, that you deal with as well as a legal description of the property. You will want to indicate the exact name that your interest is held in as well as the current value and the latest tax information. You will be given the opportunity to list any monthly/quarterly payments of income received, in **Chapter 3** under **Sources of Income.**

Note to self: _____

_____

_____

_____

✎ **Notes Receivable** – should you hold a promissory note payable to you, specify the date, borrower's name and how the debt is to be repaid. Indicate where the original documents supporting this debt may be found and place a copy in your **TCB Folder**.

I encourage individuals to never lend money to a family member or friend without a written, signed note. Needless to say, it becomes very difficult to demand payment, in settling an estate, if the agreement was verbal.

📁 **Art, Jewelry, Antiques, and Furniture** – I recommend taking pictures of all such assets and attaching either the latest appraisal and/or purchase invoice. This documentation will not only come in handy when valuing your estate but can be useful for insurance purposes as well.

You might also designate who you would like to inherit certain items by attaching an addendum to your will or simply listing (in your own handwriting) your wishes. Date and sign and make sure someone knows that this list exists and where it is located.

Documenting the history of ownership on heirloom jewelry and antiques might be appreciated by those that inherit such assets. Also note any jewelry insurance riders under **Chapter 7: Insurance**.

Note to self: _____

_____

_____

_____

_____

_____

✎ **Coin/Stamp/Other Collections** – recommend you follow the same advice for documenting other untitled assets such as those listed prior.

Note to self: _____

_____

_____

_____

_____

- 🖉 **Gold/Silver** – any gold or silver owned and held outside of an investment account should be noted along with where these valuables are kept.

- 🖉 **Guns** – note the model and registration numbers and make a notation in your documentation that because these are currently registered in your name, they cannot necessarily be transferred to another individual without re-registering. Consult your attorney on this matter if it is applicable to you.

Note to self: _____

_____

_____

_____

_____

_____

- 🖉 **List of Copyrights, Patents, & Royalties** – list specifics and place sufficient documentation in your **TCB Folder.**

Note to self: _____

_____

_____

_____

_____

_____

- 🖉 **Reward Programs** – list frequent flier miles, casino rewards, hotel rewards, etc.

Note to self: _____

_____

_____

_____

_____

✒ **Other Assets** – that need to be listed.

Note to self: _____

_____

_____

_____

_____

_____

I recall vividly a friend of mine who inherited her parent's assets including beautiful antiques and artwork. She was overwhelmed with the prospects of disposing of most of it as she had little space in her home to place everything (not to mention she was not a huge fan of antiques).

She considered having a weekend estate sale and several of her friends agreed to help. When I asked her if she planned to have certain items appraised, she rolled her eyes and dismissed my suggestion . . . that is until the first hour of the estate sale when an honest buyer informed her that she was selling a painting for much less than its real value!

He further commented that most of her antiques seemed way underpriced. She immediately shut the sale down and took the time to research and have appraisals done. The second sale netted her 3 times as much as she had initially anticipated!

It is always important for you to note in your documentation any valuable items especially those that could increase in value overtime.

ROADMAP

Personal Real Estate and Other Assets

Note: If you don't own your primary residence and are leasing/renting please indicate under property #1.

Property #1 Residence

Address of Property _____

Parish/County _____

City _____ State _____

Residence is Leased/Rented ☐ Yes ☐ No

Name of Lessor _____

Phone # _____

Amount of Lease $ _____ Terms of Lease _____

Is residence owned by you? ☐ Yes ☐ No Property Purchase Date ___ / ___ / ____

Indicate exact ownership as recorded in public records _____

_____

Community Property with Spouse ☐ Yes ☐ No

Separate Property ☐ Yes ☐ No

Relationship of Other Owners (other than spouse)

☐ Sibling ☐ Child ☐ Partner ☐ Other

If other, please specify relationship _____

Legal Description of Property _____

_____

Indicate if this property is held in a trust ☐ Yes ☐ No

Title of Trust _____

_____

Name and Contact Information of Trustee _____

_____

Is the property debt free? ☐ Yes ☐ No

Is mortgage paid in full? ☐ Yes ☐ No *If yes,* list location of the deed _____

_____

Outstanding Mortgage (list mortgage holder and address) _____

_____

Appraisal

Date of Last Appraisal ___ / ___ / _____ Appraised Value $_____

List original cost if no appraisal is available $_____

Community Homeowner Assessments

Due Date ___ / ___ / _____ Amount $_____

Due Date ___ / ___ / _____ Amount $_____

Property #2 Other

Address of Property _____

Parish/County _____

City _____ State _____

Property Purchase Date ___ / ___ / _____

Indicate exact ownership as recorded in public records _____

_____

Community Property with Spouse ☐ Yes ☐ No

Separate Property ☐ Yes ☐ No

Relationship (other than spouse) of other owners

☐ Sibling ☐ Child ☐ Partner ☐ Other

If other, please specify relationship _____

Legal Description of Property _____

_____

Indicate if this property is held in a trust ☐ Yes ☐ No

Title of Trust _____

_____

Name and Contact Information of Trustee _____

_____

Is the property debt free? ☐ Yes ☐ No

Is mortgage paid in full? ☐ Yes ☐ No *If yes,* list location of the deed _____

_____

Outstanding Mortgage (list mortgage holder and address) _____

_____

Appraisal

Date of Last Appraisal ___ / ___ / _____ Appraised Value $_____

List original cost if no appraisal is available $_____

Community Homeowner Assessments

Due Date ___ / ___ / _____ Amount $_____

Due Date ___ / ___ / _____ Amount $_____

Property #3 Other

Address of Property _____

Parish/County _____

City _____ State _____

Property Purchase Date ___ / ___ / _____

Indicate exact ownership as recorded in public records _____

_____

Community Property with Spouse ☐ Yes ☐ No

Separate Property ☐ Yes ☐ No

Relationship (other than spouse) of other owners

☐ Sibling ☐ Child ☐ Partner ☐ Other

If other, please specify relationship _____

Legal Description of Property _____

_____

Indicate if this property is held in a trust ☐ Yes ☐ No

Title of Trust _____

_____

Name and Contact Information of Trustee _____

_____

Is the property debt free? ☐ Yes ☐ No

Is mortgage paid in full? ☐ Yes ☐ No *If yes*, list location of the deed _____

_____

Outstanding Mortgage (list mortgage holder and address) _____

_____

Appraisal

Date of Last Appraisal ___ / ___ / _____ Appraised Value $_____

List original cost if no appraisal is available $_____

Community Homeowner Assessments

Due Date ___ / ___ / _____ Amount $_____

Due Date ___ / ___ / _____ Amount $_____

Property #4 Other

Address of Property _____

Parish/County _____

City _____ State _____

Property Purchase Date ___ / ___ / _____

Indicate exact ownership as recorded in public records _____

_____

Community Property with Spouse ☐ Yes ☐ No

Separate Property ☐ Yes ☐ No

Relationship (other than spouse) of other owners

☐ Sibling ☐ Child ☐ Partner ☐ Other

If other, please specify relationship _____

Legal Description of Property _____

_____

Indicate if this property is held in a trust ☐ Yes ☐ No

Title of Trust _____

_____

Name and Contact Information of Trustee _____

_____

Is the property debt free? ☐ Yes ☐ No

Is mortgage paid in full? ☐ Yes ☐ No *If yes,* list location of the deed _____

_____

Outstanding Mortgage (list mortgage holder and address) _____

_____

Appraisal

Date of Last Appraisal ___ / ___ / _____ Appraised Value $_____

List original cost if no appraisal is available $_____

Community Homeowner Assessments

Due Date ___ / ___ / _____   Amount $_____

Due Date ___ / ___ / _____   Amount $_____

Timeshares

Address of Property _____

Name of entity holding your timeshare agreement and their contact information _____

_____

_____

Exact name(s) of owners of the timeshare contract _____

_____

Date of Contract ___ / ___ / _____

Terms of Contract _____

Annual Cost $_____

A copy of the contract is included in my **TCB Folder**   ☐ Yes   ☐ No

Offsite Storage (Boats, Campers, Motor Homes, Furniture, etc.)

Name of Storage Facility _____

Address of Storage Facility _____

Leased in the Name of _____

Storage Unit # _____

Storage facility security code to enter grounds or building _____

Security Code/Combination for Storage Unit _____

Storage Unit Key Location _____

Information concerning additional storage facilities _____

_____

_____

_____

A list has been placed in my **TCB Folder** of important/valuable items in storage unit

☐ Yes   ☐ No

Vehicles

1. Make and Model _____

Name(s) on Title _____

License Plate # _____ VIN # _____

Is the vehicle financed?   ☐ Yes   ☐ No

If yes, name and address of lender _____

_____

If no, location of title _____

Is the vehicle leased?   ☐ Yes   ☐ No   Date of Lease Expiration ___ / ___ / _____

If yes, name and address of lessor _____

_____

2. Make and Model _____

Name(s) on Title _____

License Plate # _____ VIN # _____

Is the vehicle financed?   ☐ Yes   ☐ No

If yes, name and address of lender _____

_____

If no, location of title _____

Is the vehicle leased?   ☐ Yes   ☐ No   Date of Lease Expiration ___ / ___ / _____

If yes, name and address of lessor _____

_____

3. Make and Model _____

Name(s) on Title _____

License Plate # _____ VIN # _____

Is the vehicle financed? ☐ Yes ☐ No

If yes, name and address of lender _____

_____

If no, location of title _____

Is the vehicle leased? ☐ Yes ☐ No   Date of Lease Expiration ___ / ___ / _____

If yes, name and address of lessor _____

_____

Motorcycles

Make and Model _____

Name(s) on Title _____

License Plate # _____ VIN # _____

Other important information to note _____

_____

Boats

Description of Boat(s) and Trailer(s)

1. _____

Name(s) on Title _____

Trailer License Plate #_____ Boat HIN#_____

2. _____

Name(s) on Title _____

Trailer License Plate #_____ Boat HIN#_____

3. _____

Name(s) on Title _____

Trailer License Plate #_____ Boat HIN#_____

Other important information to note _____

_____

_____

Campers

Description of Camper _____

License Plate # _____ VIN # _____

Name(s) on Title _____

Camper Storage Location _____

Other important information to note _____

_____

_____

Oil, Timber, Gas, and Mineral Interests

Describe the interest or type of royalty that you own, including the location of the property and information on the company that leases from you. Be sure to include their contact information. Also indicate the exact name(s) of lease ownership.

Note any income received and the frequency of the payment in **Chapter 3: Financial.**

_____

_____

_____

_____

_____

Note Receivable

Borrower's Name _____

Borrower's Address _____

Terms of Note and Interest Rate _____

Frequency and amount of periodic payments and the due date _____

_____

Location of Original Note _____

Describe any collateral securing this debt _____

_____

Art, Jewelry, Antiques, Furniture

Indicate where original invoices, appraisals, pictures of stored items are kept. Also, note if you wish to pass on or donate any particular item(s) at some point. Document other important information considering the above assets.

_____

_____

_____

_____

_____

_____

Stamps, Other Collections

Description and Location of Collections _____

_____

_____

_____

_____

Does an appraisal exist?   ☐ Yes   ☐ No

I have included the appraisal in my **TCB Folder**   ☐ Yes   ☐ No

If no, indicate location of appraisal _____

Other important information concerning the above listed assets _____

_____

_____

_____

_____

Gold, Silver Coins (held outside of an investment account)

Description and location where assets are stored _____

_____

_____

_____

_____

Guns

1. Make and Model _____

Registered to _____

Corresponding Registration # _____

2. Make and Model _____

Registered to _____

Corresponding Registration # _____

3. Make and Model _____

Registered to _____

Corresponding Registration # _____

4. Make and Model _____

Registered to _____

Corresponding Registration # _____

Check here ☐ if more guns **not** listed here exist and information is inside your **TCB Folder.**

Copyrights, Patents, Royalties

Describe type of asset along with other important information necessary to manage the continuation of any payment interest _____

_____

_____

_____

_____

_____

Check here ☐ if documents concerning the above have been placed in your **TCB Folder**

Reward Programs Frequent flyer, hotel, etc. that may have outstanding credits or need cancelling at some point.

1. Company _____ Type of Reward _____

Account # _____ Contact _____

2. Company _____ Type of Reward _____

Account # _____ Contact _____

3. Company _____ Type of Reward _____

Account # _____ Contact _____

4. Company _____ Type of Reward _____

Account # _____ Contact _____

Other Assets Not Already Listed

_____

_____

_____

_____

_____

_____

_____

_____

_____

_____

_____

_____

Changes and Additional Information (remember to date)

Changes and Additional Information (remember to date)

CHAPTER 3
Financial

In this chapter, I've compiled a list of specifics that relate to financial matters. As mentioned before, the list described below is indicative of the most common areas for consideration and may not include everything relative to your financial situation. Likewise, some of these suggested notations may not apply to you so think through your daily life and add information of importance. Put yourself in the position of the person who will be handling your affairs someday. What would you need to know and why?

- **Bank and Advisor's** – name and contact information (don't forget to list all if you have multiple relationships).

- **Investment Company and Advisor's** – name and contact information (same as above). You may want to consider at some point introducing your children to your investment advisor.

Why do I suggest this? For a couple of reasons. First of all, you probably share more about your financial goals and concerns with this individual than other advisors you deal with. Since you obviously trust their advice, perhaps you would want them to share their expertise with the individuals that stand to inherit some of what you have accumulated. In addition, a true seasoned, client focused financial advisor will keep your philosophy on saving and investing in mind, as they advise the next generation.

- **Bank and Investment Accounts** – At the end of this Chapter, list each one along with the individual account numbers. **I recommend that you only note the last four digits and not the full account number.** That will be sufficient information to locate the account.

*Note to self:*_____

_____

_____

_____

_____

_____

🖉 **Other Financial Accounts** – list any other accounts that you might also sign on such as a business account, 529 Savings Plans for your children or grandchildren, joint account with a spouse, partner or other relative.

These all need to be documented. It is also wise to check with the bank where you hold accounts to understand their policy concerning the freezing of a **joint account** when one of the account owners dies. Ask that the policy be given to you in writing.

Note to self: _____

_____

_____

_____

_____

_____

🖉 **Trusts** – are you the beneficiary of a trust, if so, who is the trustee?

What is the trustee's contact information?

Are you a trustee of a trust, if so, where are the assets of the trust held?

Have you created trusts during your lifetime, if so, who is the trustee and what is their contact information?

🖉 **Current Income Source** – *be as specific as possible.* These might consist of salary or social security, rental income, royalties, pension or other retirement, military benefits, investment account income (such as annuities), receivables from a loan you extended to someone or business income. Referring to your tax returns will help remind you of most sources.

Note to self: _____

_____

_____

🖉 **Retirement/IRA Accounts** – include full description, account numbers and named beneficiaries.

Note to self: _____

_____

_____

_____

_____

_____

✎ **Pension Plans** – If you have a pension plan, note first whether distribution has begun. Include full description of plans, account numbers, and named beneficiaries for either future benefits or payout of any residual balance.

Note to self: _____

_____

_____

✎ **Social Security Benefits** – Note the current amount and the date direct deposit is received. If you maintain multiple checking accounts, note which one receives the deposit. If you have not yet begun taking these benefits, indicate when you anticipate doing so and update this information when applicable.

✎ **Savings Bonds and/or Stock Certificates** – list any that are not held in an account and the location of these items.

Note to self: _____

_____

_____

_____

_____

✎ **Automatic Bank Drafts** – such as monthly bills or periodic insurance premiums and automatic deposits. Also note how often they are processed: monthly, semi-annually, etc. Also be sure to include information on any bills that are automatically paid by one of your credit card accounts.

Note to self: _____

_____

_____

    🖊 **Outstanding Mortgage or Other Personal Liabilities** – such as car debt, bank loans or promissory notes that you might owe to another individual. You will be prompted (when completing the checklist) to be specific about who holds the debt, amount and frequency of payments as well as any collateral that is held until the debt is paid in full.

You should note specifically how you receive billing statements (by mail or online) and as mentioned above, whether payment is set up on automatic drafts from checking or credit card accounts. If debt is business related **AND** in the name of the business, wait. We'll address that in **Chapter 6: Business Information.**

Note to self: _____

_____

_____

    🖊 **Active Credit Cards** – and the issuer. Again, I recommend you only note the last four digits of the credit card account number. These accounts will need to be cancelled at some point and I'll explain why in **Chapter 11: Miscellaneous Things to do in Handling My Estate**

Note to self: _____

_____

_____

_____

_____

_____

    🖊 **Bankruptcy** – Note if you have ever filed bankruptcy, as well as the date, city and state of such filing. Indicate also if the bankruptcy was in personal or business name.

    🖊 **Bank Safe Deposit Box** – note the location of the box (name and address of bank) and where the key to access the box can be found. At the time the box is rented, you are provided two keys so you may decide to actually give your designee a key in advance. Remember, if you want another individual to access the box at any time (including after your death), rent the box in both names. Don't just make them an authorized signer which is similar to a *Power of Attorney* and is therefore null and void at the time of the grantor's death. Again, you need to check with your particular bank to make sure that their policy is not different. It is also recommended that you make a list of the contents of the box, especially if someone else is given accessibility in your absence.

✎ **Outstanding Philanthropic Pledges** – as you update your TCB document annually, make a note of pledges you may have made to your church or other non-profits that are outstanding and that you would want honored. Note the balance of each at the time of your update.

Note to self: _____

_____

_____

✎ **Additional Financial Information** – which you may need to document.

Note to self: _____

_____

_____

_____

While we are on the subject of financial matters, I also recommend notifying all three credit agencies (Experian, TransUnion and Equifax) once you reach the age OR financial position to no longer seek credit. This helps prevent credit fraud on your behalf. When someone steals your identity, the burden of proof is on you! You can always have your files reopened, should you decide or need to seek credit later. The process to reopen your files is easy and can be done online or with a phone call.

Note: When you have your credit files closed, you will receive confirmation from the credit agencies along with a password that allows you to easily have the files reopened!

Once you have completed taking notes for **Chapter 3**, complete the checklist that will go in your **TCB Folder**.

ROADMAP
Financial

Many couples both share and maintain individual accounts. In this section, be sure to document the exact titles the accounts are listed under. This will help determine shared and individual accounts.

Note: When listing account numbers only list the last 4 digits of the account unless otherwise specified.

Personal Savings, Checking, Money Market, Certificates of Deposit, and Investment Accounts

1. Title of Account _____ Acct # __ __ __ __

Type of Account _____

Location of Account _____

Banker/Advisor _____

Contact Information _____

2. Title of Account _____ Acct # __ __ __ __

Type of Account _____

Location of Account _____

Banker/Advisor _____

Contact Information _____

3. Title of Account _____ Acct # __ __ __ __

Type of Account _____

Location of Account _____

Banker/Advisor _____

Contact Information _____

4. Title of Account _____ Acct # __ __ __ __

Type of Account _____

Location of Account _____

Banker/Advisor _____

Contact Information _____

5. Title of Account _____ Acct # __ __ __ __

Type of Account _____

Location of Account _____

Banker/Advisor _____

Contact Information _____

6. Title of Account _____ Acct # __ __ __ __

Type of Account _____

Location of Account _____

Banker/Advisor _____

Contact Information _____

Retirement Accounts – IRA, 401K Plan

Do you have any retirement accounts? ☐ Yes ☐ No

1. Bank/Investment Company _____

Contact Person/Advisor _____

Phone # _____

Exact Title of Account _____

☐ Traditional IRA   ☐ Roth IRA   ☐ 401K Plan   Acct # __ __ __ __

Beneficiary _____

Have periodic withdrawals begun? ☐ Yes ☐ No

2. Bank/Investment Company _____

Contact Person/Advisor _____

Phone # _____

Exact Title of Account _____

☐ Traditional IRA   ☐ Roth IRA   ☐ 401K Plan   Acct # __ __ __ __

Beneficiary _____

Have periodic withdrawals begun?   ☐ Yes   ☐ No

3. Bank/Investment Company _____

Contact Person/Advisor _____

Phone # _____

Exact Title of Account _____

☐ Traditional IRA   ☐ Roth IRA   ☐ 401K Plan   Acct # __ __ __ __

Beneficiary _____

Have periodic withdrawals begun?   ☐ Yes   ☐ No

4. Bank/Investment Company _____

Contact Person/Advisor _____

Phone # _____

Exact Title of Account _____

☐ Traditional IRA   ☐ Roth IRA   ☐ 401K Plan   Acct # __ __ __ __

Beneficiary _____

Have periodic withdrawals begun?   ☐ Yes   ☐ No

Pension Plans

Do you have any pension plans? ☐ Yes ☐ No

1. Company that Established the Pension _____

Pension in the Name of _____

Pension Investment Administrator _____

Full Account # _____

Have periodic payments begun? ☐ Yes ☐ No

Are there survivor benefits under this plan? ☐ Yes ☐ No

If yes, Beneficiary's name _____

2. Company that Established the Pension _____

Pension in the Name of _____

Pension Investment Administrator _____

Full Account # _____

Have periodic payments begun? ☐ Yes ☐ No

Are there survivor benefits under this plan? ☐ Yes ☐ No

If yes, Beneficiary's name _____

3. Company that Established the Pension _____

Pension in the Name of _____

Pension Investment Administrator _____

Full Account # _____

Have periodic payments begun? ☐ Yes ☐ No

Are there survivor benefits under this plan? ☐ Yes ☐ No

If yes, Beneficiary's name _____

Annuities

Do you have any annuities? ☐ Yes ☐ No

1. Name of Issuing Company _____

Agent and Contact # _____

Account in Name(s) of _____

Full Policy # _____ Terms _____

Beneficiaries _____

2. Name of Issuing Company _____

Agent and Contact # _____

Account in Name(s) of _____

Full Policy # _____ Terms _____

Beneficiaries _____

3. Name of Issuing Company _____

Agent and Contact # _____

Account in Name(s) of _____

Full Policy # _____ Terms _____

Beneficiaries _____

Other Financial Accounts

List other non-retirement accounts such as 529 Plans.

1. Title of Account _____ Acct # __ __ __ __

Bank & Location of Account _____

Banker/Advisor _____

Contact Information _____

2. Title of Account _____ Acct # __ __ __ __

Bank & Location of Account _____

Banker/Advisor _____

Contact Information _____

3. Title of Account _____ Acct # __ __ __ __

Bank & Location of Account _____

Banker/Advisor _____

Contact Information _____

4. Title of Account _____ Acct # __ __ __ __

Bank & Location of Account _____

Banker/Advisor _____

Contact Information _____

5. Title of Account _____ Acct # __ __ __ __

Bank & Location of Account _____

Banker/Advisor _____

Contact Information _____

6. Title of Account _____ Acct # __ __ __ __

Bank & Location of Account _____

Banker/Advisor _____

Contact Information _____

Trusts – Check if applicable

1. A trust has been created ☐ Yes ☐ No

☐ Existing Outside of Will   ☐ Included in the Will

Title of Trust _____

Trust Created by _____

Name of Trustee _____

Trustee Contact Information _____

2. A second trust has been created (different from indicated above) ☐ Yes ☐ No

☐ Existing Outside of Will   ☐ Included in the Will

Title of Trust _____

Trust Created by _____

Name of Trustee _____

Trustee Contact Information _____

1. I am the **Beneficiary** of a Trust ☐ Yes ☐ No

Title of Trust _____

Name of Trustee _____

Trustee Contact Information _____

2. Spouse is the **Beneficiary** of a Trust ☐ Yes ☐ No

Title of Trust _____

Name of Trustee _____

Trustee Contact Information _____

Current Income Sources

Note: Don't be concerned about documenting amounts. Only be concerned that all sources are identified for the one who may end up caring for you. You will have the opportunity to provide more specifics later. Space is provided for two recipients.

1. Name of Recipient _____

☐ Salary   ☐ Social Security   ☐ Rental Income   ☐ Royalties

☐ Worker's Compensation   ☐ Pension   ☐ Other Retirement

☐ Military Benefits   ☐ Annuities   ☐ Note Receivable   ☐ Business Income

List Other Sources of Income (not already noted) _____

_____

2. Name of Recipient _____

☐ Salary ☐ Social Security ☐ Rental Income ☐ Royalties

☐ Worker's Compensation ☐ Pension ☐ Other Retirement

☐ Military Benefits ☐ Annuities ☐ Note Receivable ☐ Business Income

List Other Sources of Income (not already noted) _____

_____

Social Security Benefits

1. Name of Recipient _____

Have monthly benefits begun? ☐ Yes ☐ No

Approximate Date of Monthly Deposit. ___ / ___ / _____

Bank and the account receiving the direct deposit _____

Acct # __ __ __ __ Exact Title of Account _____

2. Name of Recipient _____

Have monthly benefits begun? ☐ Yes ☐ No

Approximate Date of Monthly Deposit. ___ / ___ / _____

Bank and the account receiving the direct deposit _____

Acct # __ __ __ __ Exact Title of Account _____

Savings Bonds and/or Stock Certificates (not held in an investment account)

☐ Exists ☐ Do Not Exist

1. Stock Description

Issuer of Stock _____

Certificate # _____ # of Shares _____

Name of the Owner(s) _____

Certificate Date ___ / ___ / _____

Location of Stock Certificate _____

2. Stock Description

Issuer of Stock _____

Certificate # _____ # of Shares _____

Name of the Owner(s) _____

Certificate Date ___ / ___ / _____

Location of Stock Certificate _____

3. Stock Description

Issuer of Stock _____

Certificate # _____ # of Shares _____

Name of the Owner(s) _____

Certificate Date ___ / ___ / _____

Location of Stock Certificate _____

1. Bond Description

Name of Owner(s) _____

Type of Bond _____

Face Amount $_____ Issue Date ___ / ___ / _____

Location of Bond _____

2. Bond Description

Name of Owner(s) _____

Type of Bond _____

Face Amount $_____ Issue Date ___ / ___ / _____

Location of Bond _____

Note: Indicate here if you hold a more complex list of Stocks and Bonds and have placed that list in your **TCB Folder** ☐ Yes ☐ No

Automatic Recurring Bank Drafts

☐ Exists   ☐ Do Not Exist

1. Payable to _____

On Behalf of _____

Date of Draft ___ /___ /_____ Frequency _____ Amount $_____

Purpose of Draft _____

Last 4 Digits of Acct # __ __ __ __ Bank _____

2. Payable to _____

On Behalf of _____

Date of Draft ___ /___ /_____ Frequency _____ Amount $_____

Purpose of Draft _____

Last 4 Digits of Acct # __ __ __ __ Bank _____

3. Payable to _____

On Behalf of _____

Date of Draft ___ /___ /_____ Frequency _____ Amount $_____

Purpose of Draft _____

Last 4 Digits of Acct # __ __ __ __ Bank _____

4. Payable to _____

On Behalf of _____

Date of Draft ___ /___ /_____ Frequency _____ Amount $_____

Purpose of Draft _____

Last 4 Digits of Acct # __ __ __ __ Bank _____

5. Payable to _____

On Behalf of _____

Date of Draft ___ /___ /_____ Frequency _____ Amount $_____

Purpose of Draft _____

Last 4 Digits of Acct # __ __ __ __   Bank _____

6. Payable to _____

On Behalf of _____

Date of Draft ___ / ___ / _____   Frequency _____   Amount $_____

Purpose of Draft _____

Last 4 Digits of Acct # __ __ __ __   Bank _____

Other Personal Liabilities/Debt Including Leases
(Other than Primary Residence)

☐ Exists   ☐ Do Not Exist

1. Liability Owed to _____

Address _____

Terms of Debt _____

Payment Frequency _____   Amount $_____

Name of Borrower(s) _____

Account # _____

Collateral (if any) _____

Billing Received Via   ☐ Mail   ☐ Online   Billing Email Address _____

Auto Draft   ☐ Yes   ☐ No   *If yes,* Last 4 Digits of Account # __ __ __ __

2. Liability Owed to _____

Address _____

Terms of Debt _____

Payment Frequency _____   Amount $_____

Name of Borrower(s) _____

Account # _____

Collateral (if any) _____

Billing Received Via ☐ Mail ☐ Online Billing Email Address _____

Auto Draft ☐ Yes ☐ No *If yes,* Last 4 Digits of Account # __ __ __ __

3. Liability Owed to _____

Address _____

Terms of Debt _____

Payment Frequency _____ Amount $_____

Name of Borrower(s) _____

Account # _____

Collateral (if any) _____

Billing Received Via ☐ Mail ☐ Online Billing Email Address _____

Auto Draft ☐ Yes ☐ No *If yes,* Last 4 Digits of Account # __ __ __ __

4. Liability Owed to _____

Address _____

Terms of Debt _____

Payment Frequency _____ Amount $_____

Name of Borrower(s) _____

Account # _____

Collateral (if any) _____

Billing Received Via ☐ Mail ☐ Online Billing Email Address _____

Auto Draft ☐ Yes ☐ No *If yes,* Last 4 Digits of Account # __ __ __ __

5. Liability Owed to _____

Address _____

Terms of Debt _____

Payment Frequency _____ Amount $_____

Name of Borrower(s) _____

Account # _____

Collateral (if any) _____

Billing Received Via ☐ Mail ☐ Online Billing Email Address _____

Auto Draft ☐ Yes ☐ No *If yes,* Last 4 Digits of Account # __ __ __ __

Active/Outstanding Credit and Debit Cards

Note: Recommend you close all inactive credit card accounts and shred cards

1. Card Issuer _____

Card Issuer Contact # (found on back of card) _____

Last 4 Digits of Acct # __ __ __ __   Expiration Date ____ /_____

Name on Card _____

2. Card Issuer _____

Card Issuer Contact # (found on back of card) _____

Last 4 Digits of Acct # __ __ __ __   Expiration Date ____ /_____

Name on Card _____

3. Card Issuer _____

Card Issuer Contact # (found on back of card) _____

Last 4 Digits of Acct # __ __ __ __   Expiration Date ____ /_____

Name on Card _____

4. Card Issuer _____

Card Issuer Contact # (found on back of card) _____

Last 4 Digits of Acct # __ __ __ __   Expiration Date ____ /_____

Name on Card _____

5. Card Issuer _____

Card Issuer Contact # (found on back of card) _____

Last 4 Digits of Acct # __ __ __ __   Expiration Date ____ /_____

Name on Card _____

6. Card Issuer _____

Card Issuer Contact # (found on back of card) _____

Last 4 Digits of Acct # __ __ __ __   Expiration Date ____ /_____

Name on Card _____

7. Card Issuer _____

Card Issuer Contact # (found on back of card) _____

Last 4 Digits of Acct # __ __ __ __   Expiration Date ____ /_____

Name on Card _____

8. Card Issuer _____

Card Issuer Contact # (found on back of card) _____

Last 4 Digits of Acct # __ __ __ __   Expiration Date ____ /_____

Name on Card _____

Co-Signer of Loan

☐ Yes   ☐ No

1. Name of Primary Borrower _____

Legal Name of Co-signer _____

Debt Owed to _____

Date of Loan ___ /___ /_____ Terms of Loan _____

Describe Collateral (If any) _____

Owner of Collateral Pledged to Loan _____

2. Name of Primary Borrower _____

Legal Name of Co-signer _____

Debt Owed to _____

Date of Loan ___ /___ /_____ Terms of Loan _____

Describe Collateral (If any) _____

Owner of Collateral Pledged to Loan _____

Bankruptcy Filing History

Have you ever filed bankruptcy? ☐ Yes ☐ No

If yes, Date of Filing ___ / ___ / _____ Type of Bankruptcy _____

City and State _____

Was the bankruptcy ☐ Personal ☐ Business

Name of Debtor _____

Has the bankruptcy been settled? ☐ Yes ☐ No *If no*, list the contact information
for the Trustee _____

Additional bankruptcy pertinent to this Roadmap ☐ Yes ☐ No

If yes, Date of Filing ___ / ___ / _____ Type of Bankruptcy _____

City and State _____

Was the bankruptcy ☐ Personal ☐ Business

Name of Debtor _____

Has the bankruptcy been settled? ☐ Yes ☐ No *If no*, list the contact information
for the Trustee _____

Outstanding Lawsuits/Judgements

Do you have any outstanding lawsuits or judgements? ☐ Yes ☐ No

Representing Attorney _____

Describe the nature of the lawsuit or judgement _____

_____

_____

_____

_____

_____

_____

Bank Safe Deposit Box

Do you have a safe deposit box? ☐ Yes ☐ No

1. Box Rented in the Name of _____

Bank Location _____

_____

Box # _____ Location of Keys _____

Person(s) Authorized to Access Box _____

Box Inventory _____

_____

_____

_____

_____

_____

Are there additional safe deposit boxes? ☐ Yes ☐ No

2. Box Rented in the Name of _____

Bank Location _____

_____

Box # _____ Location of Keys _____

Person(s) Authorized to Access Box _____

Box Inventory _____

_____

_____

_____

_____

_____

Outstanding Philanthropic Pledges

Do you have any outstanding philanthropic pledges?   ☐ Yes   ☐ No

1. Payable to _____

Name of Donor(s) _____

Terms of Pledge (start and end date) _____

Total Amount Outstanding $_____

2. Payable to _____

Name of Donor(s) _____

Terms of Pledge (start and end date) _____

Total Amount Outstanding $_____

3. Payable to _____

Name of Donor(s) _____

Terms of Pledge (start and end date) _____

Total Amount Outstanding $_____

4. Payable to _____

Name of Donor(s) _____

Terms of Pledge (start and end date) _____

Total Amount Outstanding $_____

Additional Financial Information

_____

_____

_____

_____

_____

_____

Changes and Additional Information (remember to date)

Changes and Additional Information (remember to date)

CHAPTER 4
Memberships, Contracts, Service Providers

It is helpful to document this information not only for a caregiver to know who to contact if need be, but also necessary to know what to cancel when settling your affairs. This is just a sample, you may have others.

- **Health or Fitness Clubs** – list location, any membership numbers and cost. Also note if the charges are debited from an account monthly or periodically billed.

- **Country Club or other Social Memberships** – that have dues and may need to be cancelled at some point. Note if there was a purchase of stock associated with membership, which could be sold or transferred to others.

- **Magazine, Digital, Pet, Clothing, Food or Wine Subscriptions** – provide details on type, provider, how paid for and frequency of mail orders. These would also need to be addressed if you move.

Note to self: _____

_____

_____

- **Cable, Computer, Phone (Cell, Home or Business) Alarm, Daily Newspaper, Dry Cleaning Delivery** – list providers to enable contact for service and/or cancellation at some point.

Note to self: _____

_____

_____

_____

_____

_____

- ✎ **Maid or Lawn Service Providers** – that you routinely employ to service your home's maintenance.

- ✎ **Other Repair or Service Providers** – List your preference for providers that you want taking care of your home and property in case someone would have to initiate this for you. Examples might be gardener, plumber, electrician, painter, exterminator, computer service provider, alarm or other security provider, etc. If you have signed annual contracts with any maintenance or service providers, place copies of the contracts in the **TCB Folder**.

Note to self: _____

_____

_____

_____

_____

_____

- ✎ **Other Contracts or Memberships** – not listed above but applicable to your circumstances.

Note to self: _____

_____

_____

_____

_____

_____

Once you have completed taking notes for **Chapter 4**, complete the section that will go in your **TCB Folder**.

ROADMAP

Memberships, Contracts, Service Providers

Health or Fitness Clubs

1. Member's Name(s) _____

Name and Address of Club _____

_____

Membership # _____ Fees $_____

Fees are paid by ☐ Mail ☐ Auto Debit If debited, list last 4 digits of acct# __ __ __ __

Name on Bank Acct Auto Debited _____

2. Member's Name(s) _____

Name and Address of Club _____

_____

Membership # _____ Fees $_____

Fees are paid by ☐ Mail ☐ Auto Debit If debited, list last 4 digits of acct# __ __ __ __

Name on Bank Acct Auto Debited _____

Country Club or Social Memberships

Name and Address of Club _____

_____

Membership # _____ Fees $_____

Fees are paid by ☐ Mail ☐ Auto Debit If debited, list last 4 digits of acct# __ __ __ __

Name on Bank Acct Auto Debited _____

Stock Issued ☐ Yes ☐ No   Is stock transferrable? ☐ Yes ☐ No

Original Cost $_____   Is stock eligible for resale ☐ Yes ☐ No

Magazine, Digital, Pet, Clothing, Food or Wine Subscriptions, Other Outstanding Periodic Subscriptions

1. Subscription _____ Type _____

Frequency _____ Payment Method _____

2. Subscription _____ Type _____

Frequency _____ Payment Method _____

3. Subscription _____ Type _____

Frequency _____ Payment Method _____

4. Subscription _____ Type _____

Frequency _____ Payment Method _____

Provider Services

Cable Provider _____

Frequency _____ Payment Method _____

Internet Provider _____

Frequency _____ Payment Method _____

Cell Phone Provider _____

Frequency _____ Payment Method _____

Home Phone Provider _____

Frequency _____ Payment Method _____

Alarm Services _____

Frequency _____ Payment Method _____

Exterminator Services _____

Frequency _____ Payment Method _____

Daily Newspaper _____

Frequency _____ Payment Method _____

Dry Cleaning Delivery _____

Frequency _____ Payment Method _____

Additional Providers Services

1. Type of Service _____

Provider Name _____

Frequency _____ Payment Method _____

2. Type of Service _____

Provider Name _____

Frequency _____ Payment Method _____

3. Type of Service _____

Provider Name _____

Frequency _____ Payment Method _____

Individual Home Service Providers

Housekeeper _____

Contact Information _____

Lawn Care _____

Contact Information _____

Plumber _____

Contact Information _____

Electrician _____

Contact Information _____

Painter _____

Contact Information _____

Computer Services _____

Contact Information _____

Additional Home Service Providers

1. Type of Service _____

Provider Name _____

Contact Information _____

2. Type of Service _____

Provider Name _____

Contact Information _____

3. Type of Service _____

Provider Name _____

Contact Information _____

Other Contracts and Memberships

_____

_____

_____

_____

_____

_____

Changes and Additional Information (remember to date)

Changes and Additional Information (remember to date)

CHAPTER 5
Medical

The documentation of information concerning your health and future wishes is one of the most important topics to share, especially if someone other than a spouse/partner has to step in and care for you. When I mentioned updating changes, this is an area of particular importance. Note the following information that should be included.

- **Physician's Names, Phone Numbers and Locations** – remember to include ALL specialist that manage your health including dental and eye care.

- **Current Medical and Dental Conditions** – which you are being treated for.

- **List Medications** – that you are currently taking. Be specific, include prescribed medications and over the counter treatments. List medications for both you and your spouse if applicable.

Note to self: _____

_____

_____

_____

_____

- **Drug Allergies** – list any medications that you and/or your spouse cannot take or have reactions to.

- **Food Allergies** – also note if you and/or your spouse are glucose intolerant

- **Blood Type**

- **Hospital Preference** – in case you are unable to specify in an emergency.

- **List of Past Surgeries or Medical Conditions**

- **List any Family History of Certain Diseases or Conditions**

- **Health Insurance** – Agent and Policy numbers (wait and note under **Chapter 7: Insurance**)

- ✒ **Long Term Care Insurance** – Agent and Policy Numbers (wait and note under **Chapter 7: Insurance**)

- ✒ **State Your Wishes for Long Term Care** – Even if you don't know what your options are at this point, you can still indicate whether you would prefer to remain at home with professional sitters or are willing to go into a long-term care facility. Often the options are limited based on financial capacity or insurance coverage.

- ✒ **Medical POA (Power of Attorney)** – If this is something you have not addressed; I recommend doing so sooner than later! Most attorneys will discuss this with you when you create or update your will. Once it has been created, note the date of such document and where it is recorded (This information can be found on your copy). An original copy should also be placed in the **TCB Folder** created as part of this process.

- ✒ **Living Will** – Same as a DNR (Do Not Resuscitate). This document can be created by your attorney and is legally recorded/filed similar to a Medical Power of Attorney. You will want to note if such a document exists and the date and filing information as mentioned above. It is also a good idea to place a copy on file with your primary physician.

- ✒ **Ambulance Services Membership** – Some ambulance companies sell annual memberships. You will want to note if you own one and provide any pertinent information such as the name of the company and your membership number.

- ✒ **Additional Information Relative to your Health and Medical Care**

Note to self: _____

_____

_____

_____

_____

_____

_____

Often as we retire and age, we find ourselves relocating to be closer to family that will help look after us. That means leaving physicians and other care givers that know us and that we are comfortable with.

As you make such changes, it is always helpful to discuss your preferences for care and what you liked about your previous healthcare providers and the facilities you used.

Do some research, visit surrounding hospitals and establish a relationship with recommended specialists, physicians . . . *before* you need them!

ROADMAP

Medical

List your current medical conditions and month and year of diagnosis.

_____ ____ / _____

_____ ____ / _____

_____ ____ / _____

_____ ____ / _____

Spouse's current medical conditions and month and year of diagnosis.
(if applicable)

_____ ____ / _____

_____ ____ / _____

_____ ____ / _____

_____ ____ / _____

Your past surgeries, include month and year of surgery.

_____ ____ / _____

_____ ____ / _____

_____ ____ / _____

_____ ____ / _____

Spouse's past surgeries and month and year of surgery. (if applicable)

_____ ____ / _____

_____ ____ / _____

_____ ____ / _____

_____ ____ / _____

Family history of certain diseases or conditions

_____

_____

_____

_____

_____

_____

Spouse's family history of certain diseases or conditions. (if applicable)

_____

_____

_____

_____

_____

_____

Physician Information. Including all specialists such as dental, eye care.

1. Name of Physician _____

Contact Information _____

Type of Treatment _____

Member of Family Treated _____

2. Name of Physician _____

Contact Information _____

Type of Treatment _____

Member of Family Treated _____

3. Name of Physician _____

Contact Information _____

Type of Treatment _____

Member of Family Treated _____

4. Name of Physician _____

Contact Information _____

Type of Treatment _____

Member of Family Treated _____

5. Name of Physician _____

Contact Information _____

Type of Treatment _____

Member of Family Treated _____

6. Name of Physician _____

Contact Information _____

Type of Treatment _____

Member of Family Treated _____

7. Name of Physician _____

Contact Information _____

Type of Treatment _____

Member of Family Treated _____

8. Name of Physician _____

Contact Information _____

Type of Treatment _____

Member of Family Treated _____

Current list of medications that you take. List prescriptions and over the counter medications.

1. Medication _____ Dosage _____

Frequency _____ Rx # & Supplier _____

2. Medication _____ Dosage _____

Frequency _____ Rx # & Supplier _____

3. Medication _____ Dosage _____

Frequency _____ Rx # & Supplier _____

4. Medication _____ Dosage _____

Frequency _____ Rx # & Supplier _____

5. Medication _____ Dosage _____

Frequency _____ Rx # & Supplier _____

6. Medication _____ Dosage _____

Frequency _____ Rx # & Supplier _____

7. Medication _____ Dosage _____

Frequency _____ Rx # & Supplier _____

8. Medication _____ Dosage _____

Frequency _____ Rx # & Supplier _____

List any medications you cannot take.

_____

_____

_____

Current list of medications that your spouse takes. List prescriptions and over the counter medications.

1. Medication _____ Dosage _____

Frequency _____ Rx # & Supplier _____

2. Medication _____ Dosage _____

Frequency _____ Rx # & Supplier _____

3. Medication _____ Dosage _____

Frequency _____ Rx # & Supplier _____

4. Medication _____ Dosage _____

Frequency _____ Rx # & Supplier _____

5. Medication _____ Dosage _____

Frequency _____ Rx # & Supplier _____

6. Medication _____ Dosage _____

Frequency _____ Rx # & Supplier _____

7. Medication _____ Dosage _____

Frequency _____ Rx # & Supplier _____

8. Medication _____ Dosage _____

Frequency _____ Rx # & Supplier _____

List any medications your spouse cannot take.

_____

_____

_____

Food Allergies

_____

_____

_____

Food Allergies for Your Spouse

_____

_____

_____

Blood Type

You _____   Spouse _____

Organ Donor

You ☐ Yes ☐ No   Spouse ☐ Yes ☐ No

Hospital Preference

You _____   Spouse _____

State your wishes for long-term care

You _____

_____

Spouse _____

_____

Medical Power of Attorney

You

Name of Person Appointed _____

Relationship _____ Date of Document ___ / ___ / ___

Location of Document _____

Spouse

Name of Person Appointed _____

Relationship _____ Date of Document ___ / ___ / ___

Location of Document _____

Living Will

Do you have a living will? ☐ Yes ☐ No

If yes, location of document _____

Date of Document ___ / ___ / _____

Does your spouse have a living will? ☐ Yes ☐ No

If yes, location of document _____

Date of Document ___ / ___ / _____

Ambulance Service Membership

Name of Provider _____

Membership Details _____

Additional information relative to healthcare for you and your spouse.

_____

_____

_____

_____

Changes and Additional Information (remember to date)

Changes and Additional Information (remember to date)

CHAPTER 6
Business Information

Addressing personal affairs becomes even more complex for your loved ones when you own or have an interest in a business. That is why it is so important that you leave a roadmap for someone to follow.

- **Name of business and whether it is a Sole Proprietorship, LLC, Partnership, S-Corp or Corporation.**

- **Percentage of Ownership** – 100% or partial

- **Operating Agreement (or bylaws)** – note if one exists and where agreement can be found. If there is a Buy/Sell Agreement, so note and include a copy in the **TCB Folder.**

- **Partners or Other Shareholders** – if partners or shareholder do exist, list their full names, contact information and or note where this information can be obtained.

- **Officers** – of the business if applicable.

- **Location/Mailing Address and Important Phone Numbers** – of any and all businesses.

- **Attorney** – Name and contact information of the professional(s) that represents the business.

- **CPA** – Name and contact information of the professional that represents the business.

- **Assets** – State general information concerning assets of the business including any office building, equipment or other real estate. Indicate whether your CPA (or any other individual) can provide more detailed information as needed.

Note to self: _____

_____

_____

_____

_____

_____

🖊 **Debt** – Details of any outstanding debt or give instructions to refer to the latest financial statements on the business.

Include a copy of the most recent year end statement or tax return in your **TCB Folder.**

Note to self: _____

_____

_____

_____

_____

_____

🖊 **Accounts Receivable** – if you are a sole proprietor and this information is not a part of financials prepared by a CPA, indicate how you track such information and where it can be found.

Note: Be sure to keep it current at all times.

Note to self: _____

_____

_____

_____

_____

_____

🖊 **Partnership or Corporate Agreements** – list where originals are legally filed or can be located.

🖊 **Additional Information Related to Your Business.**

Note to self: _____

_____

_____

_____

_____

_____

It is extremely important to let your heirs know what your wishes are for the future of your business. *Example*: Sell it, continue to operate it or perhaps bring in key employees, etc. This may be including in your business succession planning documents or buy-sell agreements. You may also include instructions in your will.

Perhaps a child or family member works in your business which always makes it helpful, but if not, consider introducing them to your business partners and/or associates.

ROADMAP
Business Information

Business # 1

Name of Business _____

Physical Address _____

City _____ State _____ Zip _____

Mailing Address _____

City _____ State _____ Zip _____

Phone # _____

Legal Structure _____

Where legal business forms for this entity are recorded/filed

City _____ State _____

Ownership

1. Name _____ Ownership % _____

Phone #_____ Email _____

2. Name _____ Ownership % _____

Phone #_____ Email _____

3. Name _____ Ownership % _____

Phone #_____ Email _____

4. Name _____ Ownership % _____

Phone #_____ Email _____

Officers of Business, if applicable _____

_____

_____

_____

_____

Business Attorney and Contact Information _____

_____

_____

Business CPA and Contact Information _____

_____

_____

Assets of Business (indicate best source of this information) _____

_____

_____

Liabilities/Debts of Business (indicate the best source of this information)

_____

_____

Accounts Receivable (indicate the best source of this information and/or how you track it if you are a sole proprietor)

_____

_____

Indicate your plans or wishes for the continuation of this business beyond your involvement

_____

_____

_____

_____

_____

_____

Additional Information Related to Business

_____

_____

_____

_____

_____

_____

Business # 2

Name of Business _____

Physical Address _____

City _____ State _____ Zip _____

Mailing Address _____

City _____ State _____ Zip _____

Phone # _____

Legal Structure _____

Where legal business forms for this entity are recorded/filed

City _____ State _____

Ownership

1. Name _____ Ownership % _____

Phone #_____ Email _____

2. Name _____ Ownership % _____

Phone #_____ Email _____

3. Name _____ Ownership % _____

Phone #_____ Email _____

4. Name _____ Ownership % _____

Phone #_____ Email _____

Officers of Business, if applicable _____

_____

_____

_____

_____

Business Attorney and Contact Information _____

_____

_____

Business CPA and Contact Information _____

_____

_____

Assets of Business (indicate best source of this information) _____

_____

_____

Liabilities/Debts of Business (indicate the best source of this information)

_____

_____

Accounts Receivable (indicate the best source of this information and/or how you track it if you are a sole proprietor)

_____

_____

Indicate your plans or wishes for the continuation of this business beyond your involvement

_____

_____

_____

_____

_____

_____

Additional Information Related to Business

_____

_____

_____

_____

_____

_____

Business #3

Name of Business _____

Physical Address _____

City _____ State _____ Zip _____

Mailing Address _____

City _____ State _____ Zip _____

Phone # _____

Legal Structure _____

Where legal business forms for this entity are recorded/filed

City _____ State _____

Ownership

1. Name _____ Ownership % _____

Phone #_____ Email _____

2. Name _____ Ownership % _____

Phone #_____ Email _____

3. Name _____ Ownership % _____

Phone # _____ Email _____

4. Name _____ Ownership % _____

Phone # _____ Email _____

Officers of Business, if applicable _____

_____

_____

_____

Business Attorney and Contact Information _____

_____

_____

Business CPA and Contact Information _____

_____

_____

Assets of Business (indicate best source of this information) _____

_____

_____

Liabilities/Debts of Business (indicate the best source of this information)

_____

_____

Accounts Receivable (indicate the best source of this information and/or how you track it if you are a sole proprietor)

_____

_____

Indicate your plans or wishes for the continuation of this business beyond your involvement

_____

_____

_____

_____

_____

Additional Information Related to Business

_____

_____

_____

_____

_____

Business #4

Name of Business _____

Physical Address _____

City _____ State _____ Zip _____

Mailing Address _____

City _____ State _____ Zip _____

Phone # _____

Legal Structure _____

Where legal business forms for this entity are recorded/filed

City _____ State _____

Ownership

1. Name _____ Ownership % _____

Phone #_____ Email _____

2. Name _____ Ownership % _____

Phone #_____ Email _____

3. Name _____ Ownership % _____

Phone #_____ Email _____

4. Name _____ Ownership % _____

Phone #_____ Email _____

Officers of Business, if applicable _____

_____

_____

_____

_____

Business Attorney and Contact Information _____

_____

_____

Business CPA and Contact Information _____

_____

_____

Assets of Business (indicate best source of this information) _____

_____

_____

Liabilities/Debts of Business (indicate the best source of this information)

_____

_____

Accounts Receivable (indicate the best source of this information and/or how you track it if you are a sole proprietor)

_____

_____

Indicate your plans or wishes for the continuation of this business beyond your involvement

_____

_____

_____

_____

_____

_____

Additional Information Related to Business

_____

_____

_____

_____

_____

_____

Changes and Additional Information (remember to date)

Changes and Additional Information (remember to date)

CHAPTER 7

Insurance

With each type of insurance that is relative to you and your household be sure to list the name of the company and the agent(s) as well as their contact information and the individual policy numbers.

> 🖋 **Homeowner's Insurance (including flood)** – don't forget about renter's insurance if you rent your residence, or insurance you may carry to cover a loss that happens in offsite rented space. Also, note any policy riders for jewelry, etc.

Note to self: _____

_____

_____

> 🖋 **Vehicle Insurance** – remember to note any insurance coverage for boats, trailers, motorcycles or motorhomes in addition to your cars.

Note to self: _____

_____

_____

> 🖋 **Life Insurance** – note whether the policy is whole life or term. Also note if it is paid in full or has cash value. Specify the beneficiary.

Note to self: _____

_____

_____

> 🖋 **Health Insurance** – be sure to specify whether your insurance is through your employer or a separate policy you own. If you are on Medicare, specify the coverage you carry such as Part B & D and whether you are covered for dental and vision. Consider putting a copy of your insurance card in your **TCB Folder.**

Note to self: _____

_____

_____

✎ **Long-Term Care** – the older we get the more expensive long-term care becomes. Check with your life insurance agent to discuss the availability of Life Insurance policies that convert to long term care if needed. You may end up using part of the death benefits (for care) but the advantage is that your premiums aren't wasted as would be the case if you purchased long-term care and never used it!

Note to self: _____

_____

_____

✎ **Disability Insurance** – Be sure to specify whether it is through your employer or a separate policy you own.

Note to self: _____

_____

_____

✎ **Cancer or Intensive Care Insurance** – these typically pay a portion of your hospital stay plus chemo and radiation treatments, or if you are cared for in an ICU (Intensive Care Unit).

Note to self: _____

_____

_____

✎ **Dental and/or Vision Insurance** – note if these are separate policies or part of Medicare Coverage.

Note to self: _____

_____

_____

🖊 **Burial Insurance** – note the provider and policy number. Make sure if the policy was sold to you by a specific funeral home that the policy is **NOT** payable to that entity.

Note: Doing so may ultimately impose restrictions on using another provider for these services when the time comes. You should name your own beneficiary, perhaps your children or the individual(s) that you deem appropriate to handle your other affairs.

🖊 **Other Insurance Coverage** – not already listed

Note to self: _____

_____

_____

ROADMAP

Insurance

Home Insurance

Property #1

Name of Policy Holder(s) _____

Address of Property _____

Name of Insurance Company _____

Policy # _____

Agent's Name _____

Contact Information _____

Premium Due Date(s) ___ / ___ / _____   ___ / ___ / _____

☐ Paid Annually   ☐ Paid Bi-annually   ☐ Paid Quarterly   ☐ Paid Monthly

Check if Applicable:

☐ Renter's Insurance Only   ☐ Flood Insurance   ☐ Jewelry Rider

☐ Other Riders   Describe _____

Property #2

Name of Policy Holder(s) _____

Address of Property _____

Name of Insurance Company _____

Policy # _____

Agent's Name _____

Contact Information _____

Premium Due Date(s) ___ / ___ / _____   ___ / ___ / _____

☐ Paid Annually   ☐ Paid Bi-annually   ☐ Paid Quarterly   ☐ Paid Monthly

Check if Applicable:

☐ Renter's Insurance Only   ☐ Flood Insurance   ☐ Jewelry Rider

☐ Other Riders   Describe _____

Property #3

Name of Policy Holder(s) _____

Address of Property _____

Name of Insurance Company _____

Policy # _____

Agent's Name _____

Contact Information _____

Premium Due Date(s) ___ / ___ / _____   ___ / ___ / _____

☐ Paid Annually   ☐ Paid Bi-annually   ☐ Paid Quarterly   ☐ Paid Monthly

Check if Applicable:

☐ Renter's Insurance Only   ☐ Flood Insurance   ☐ Jewelry Rider

☐ Other Riders   Describe _____

Property #4

Name of Policy Holder(s) _____

Address of Property _____

Name of Insurance Company _____

Policy # _____

Agent's Name _____

Contact Information _____

Premium Due Date(s) ___ / ___ / _____   ___ / ___ / _____

☐ Paid Annually   ☐ Paid Bi-annually   ☐ Paid Quarterly   ☐ Paid Monthly

Check if Applicable:

☐ Renter's Insurance Only   ☐ Flood Insurance   ☐ Jewelry Rider

☐ Other Riders   Describe _____

Vehicle Insurance

Note: Indicate whether vehicle is a car, boat, trailer, motorhome, motorcycle, etc.

Vehicle #1

Name of Policy Holder(s) _____

Description of Vehicle _____

Name of Insurance Company _____

Policy # _____

Agent's Name _____

Contact Information _____

Premium Due Date(s) _____

Method of Payment _____

Vehicle #2

Name of Policy Holder(s) _____

Description of Vehicle _____

Name of Insurance Company _____

Policy # _____

Agent's Name _____

Contact Information _____

Premium Due Date(s) _____

Method of Payment _____

Vehicle #3

Name of Policy Holder(s) _____

Description of Vehicle _____

Name of Insurance Company _____

Policy # _____

Agent's Name _____

Contact Information _____

Premium Due Date(s) _____

Method of Payment _____

Vehicle #4

Name of Policy Holder(s) _____

Description of Vehicle _____

Name of Insurance Company _____

Policy # _____

Agent's Name _____

Contact Information _____

Premium Due Date(s) _____

Method of Payment _____

Vehicle #5

Name of Policy Holder(s) _____

Description of Vehicle _____

Name of Insurance Company _____

Policy # _____

Agent's Name _____

Contact Information _____

Premium Due Date(s) _____

Method of Payment _____

Vehicle #6

Name of Policy Holder(s) _____

Description of Vehicle _____

Name of Insurance Company _____

Policy # _____

Agent's Name _____

Contact Information _____

Premium Due Date(s) _____

Method of Payment _____

Life Insurance

Policy #1

Name of Policy Owner _____

Name of Insured _____

Face Value of Policy _____

Name of Insurance Company _____

Policy # _____

Agent's Name _____

Contact Information _____

Beneficiaries _____

Annual Premium $_____ Due Date(s) _____

Auto Debit (last four digits of account # __ __ __ __)

Check all that are applicable:

☐ Whole/Perm Life ☐ Term Life ☐ Cash Value ☐ Paid in Full

☐ Long-term Care Benefits Included ☐ Outstanding Policy Loans

☐ Waiver of Premium Based on Approved Disability ☐ Accidental Death

Policy #2

Name of Policy Owner _____

Name of Insured _____

Face Value of Policy _____

Name of Insurance Company _____

Policy # _____

Agent's Name _____

Contact Information _____

Beneficiaries _____

Annual Premium $_____ Due Date(s) _____

Auto Debit (last four digits of account # __ __ __ __)

Check all that are applicable:

☐ Whole/Perm Life   ☐ Term Life   ☐ Cash Value   ☐ Paid in Full

☐ Long-term Care Benefits Included   ☐ Outstanding Policy Loans

☐ Waiver of Premium Based on Approved Disability   ☐ Accidental Death

Policy #3

Name of Policy Owner _____

Name of Insured _____

Face Value of Policy _____

Name of Insurance Company _____

Policy # _____

Agent's Name _____

Contact Information _____

Beneficiaries _____

Annual Premium $_____ Due Date(s) _____

Auto Debit (last four digits of account # __ __ __ __)

Check all that are applicable:

☐ Whole/Perm Life   ☐ Term Life   ☐ Cash Value   ☐ Paid in Full

☐ Long-term Care Benefits Included   ☐ Outstanding Policy Loans

☐ Waiver of Premium Based on Approved Disability   ☐ Accidental Death

Policy #4

Name of Policy Owner _____

Name of Insured _____

Face Value of Policy _____

Name of Insurance Company _____

Policy # _____

Agent's Name _____

Contact Information _____

Beneficiaries _____

Annual Premium $_____ Due Date(s) _____

Auto Debit (last four digits of account # __ __ __ __)

Check all that are applicable:

☐ Whole/Perm Life   ☐ Term Life   ☐ Cash Value   ☐ Paid in Full

☐ Long-term Care Benefits Included   ☐ Outstanding Policy Loans

☐ Waiver of Premium Based on Approved Disability   ☐ Accidental Death

Health Insurance

Policy #1

Name of Insured _____

Name of Policy Holder _____

Name of Insurance Company _____

Policy # _____

Agent's Name _____

Contact Information _____

Indicate when and how premiums are paid _____

Check where applicable:

☐ Insurance Through Employer   ☐ Independently Held

☐ Concierge Health Care Service Provider

Physician's name and contact information _____

_____

Medicare (state all covered parts including dental and vision) _____

_____

Policy #2

Name of Insured _____

Name of Policy Holder _____

Name of Insurance Company _____

Policy # _____

Agent's Name _____

Contact Information _____

Indicate when and how premiums are paid _____

Check where applicable:

☐ Insurance Through Employer   ☐ Independently Held

☐ Concierge Health Care Service Provider

Physician's name and contact information _____

_____

Medicare (state all covered parts including dental and vision) _____

_____

Long-Term Care (not part of a life insurance policy previously listed)

Policy #1

Name of Insured _____

Name of Policy Holder _____

Name of Insurance Company _____

Policy # _____

Agent's Name _____

Contact Information _____

Indicate when and how premiums are paid _____

Policy #2

Name of Insured _____

Name of Policy Holder _____

Name of Insurance Company _____

Policy # _____

Agent's Name _____

Contact Information _____

Indicate when and how premiums are paid _____

Disability Insurance

Policy #1

Name of Insured _____

Name of Policy Holder _____

Name of Insurance Company _____

Policy # _____

Agent's Name _____

Contact Information _____

☐ Offered Through Employer   ☐ Independently Owned

Indicate when and how premiums are paid _____

Beneficiaries of survivor benefits if applicable _____

Policy #2

Name of Insured _____

Name of Policy Holder _____

Name of Insurance Company _____

Policy # _____

Agent's Name _____

Contact Information _____

☐ Offered Through Employer   ☐ Independently Owned

Indicate when and how premiums are paid _____

Beneficiaries of survivor benefits if applicable _____

Cancer or Intensive Care Insurance

Policy #1

Name of Insured _____

Name of Policy Holder _____

Type of Coverage _____

Name of Insurance Company _____

Policy # _____

Agent's Name _____

Contact Information _____

Indicate when and how premiums are paid _____

Policy #2

Name of Insured _____

Name of Policy Holder _____

Type of Coverage _____

Name of Insurance Company _____

Policy # _____

Agent's Name _____

Contact Information _____

Indicate when and how premiums are paid _____

Policy #3

Name of Insured _____

Name of Policy Holder _____

Type of Coverage _____

Name of Insurance Company _____

Policy # _____

Agent's Name _____

Contact Information _____

Indicate when and how premiums are paid _____

Policy #4

Name of Insured _____

Name of Policy Holder _____

Type of Coverage _____

Name of Insurance Company _____

Policy # _____

Agent's Name _____

Contact Information _____

Indicate when and how premiums are paid _____

Dental and/or Vision Insurance   Provide information below if you have this type of coverage and it is NOT included in insurance plans listed previously.

Policy #1

Name of Insured _____

Policy Holder _____

Type of Coverage _____

Name of Insurance Company _____

Policy # _____

Agent's Name _____

Contact Information _____

Indicate when and how premiums are paid _____

Policy #2

Name of Insured _____

Policy Holder _____

Type of Coverage _____

Name of Insurance Company _____

Policy # _____

Agent's Name _____

Contact Information _____

Indicate when and how premiums are paid _____

Policy #3

Name of Insured _____

Policy Holder _____

Type of Coverage _____

Name of Insurance Company _____

Policy # _____

Agent's Name _____

Contact Information _____

Indicate when and how premiums are paid _____

Policy #4

Name of Insured _____

Policy Holder _____

Type of Coverage _____

Name of Insurance Company _____

Policy # _____

Agent's Name _____

Contact Information _____

Indicate when and how premiums are paid _____

Funeral/Burial Insurance

Note: Sometimes funeral insurance is sold by funeral home providers and that entity is named as the beneficiary.

Policy #1

Name of Insured _____

Amount of Insurance $_____

Name of Insurance Company _____

Policy # _____

Agent's Name _____

Contact Information _____

Beneficiaries _____

Indicate when and how premiums are paid _____

Is the policy paid in full? ☐ Yes ☐ No

Policy #2

Name of Insured _____

Amount of Insurance $_____

Name of Insurance Company _____

Policy # _____

Agent's Name _____

Contact Information _____

Beneficiaries _____

Indicate when and how premiums are paid _____

Is the policy paid in full?　☐ Yes　☐ No

Information Concerning Other Insurance Coverage Not Already Listed

_____

_____

_____

_____

_____

_____

Note: Consider placing copies of all policies listed above in your **TCB Folder.**

Changes and Additional Information (remember to date)

Changes and Additional Information (remember to date)

Changes and Additional Information (remember to date)

CHAPTER 8

Taxes

I recommend you include tax information concerning both your personal returns as well as those for any business where you have ownership. You are going to want to include details such as:

📁 **CPA or Person** – who typically prepares your tax returns, as well as their contact information. If you prepare your own and use Turbo Tax or other online programs, it is a good idea to always print a copy for your files.

Also, consider providing written documentation of your online tax service user name and password for accessing prior returns.

🖊 **Federal and State Returns** – note whether all tax filings for both federal and state (if applicable) are current. Indicate if you were required to re-file any recent returns and if so, for what reason.

Also, note if you make quarterly estimated tax payments. Indicate if your CPA facilitates this on your behalf.

Note to self: _____

_____

_____

📁 **Previous Year's Return** – place a copy of the latest year's tax return in the **TCB Folder** with other crucial documents.

🖊 **Tax Audits** – if you are being audited by the IRS, indicate such and for which year(s).

🖊 **Past Returns** – indicate where past returns are stored or kept in case they are needed for future reference.

🖊 **Current Year's Return** – indicate where you accumulate information during the year (ex. Canceled checks or letters acknowledging taxable donations, etc.).

Note where this information is kept. For a more complex financial situation, explain in writing your record retention system.

- 🖊 **Property Taxes** – Make a note of any property taxes that you pay and when they are due. Note how these are typically paid (*i.e.* via payment upon billing or through escrows if properties are mortgaged).

- 🖊 **Other Tax Information** – List anything else that should be noted.

Note to self: _____

_____

_____

_____

_____

_____

This sometimes is one of the hardest areas for a loved one or friend to coordinate after you are gone. Your tax situation can be simple or extremely complex. The more difficult your situation, the more important it is to establish documentation and keep good records as the year progresses.

I suggest keeping a Tax Folder in your desk and accumulating information all during the year. Whether it is a cancelled check or bank statement indicating a donation that will be tax deductible; copies of medical copays; invoices for property taxes; etc. As the year progresses, collect information that you know will be needed at tax time.

ROADMAP

Taxes

This section may need periodic updates to your information as your life situation changes.

Personal Tax Returns (space is provided on the next page if household members file separate returns)

Full Names(s) on most recent tax returns _____

_____

Indicate which filings are applicable to your household

☐ Federal   ☐ State

Name of Tax Return Preparer _____

Preparer's Contact Information _____

Do you prepare your own taxes online?   ☐ Yes   ☐ No

Note where online access, user name, password, and PIN information is located _____

_____

Location of copies of past tax returns _____

Do you keep an accumulation file for *Current Year's* tax information?   ☐ Yes   ☐ No

If yes, where is the file located? _____

Are all income tax filings current?   ☐ Yes   ☐ No

Have you recently had to refile a tax return?   ☐ Yes   ☐ No

If yes, is the refiling   ☐ Federal and/or ☐ State List the tax year(s) _____

What is the reason for the refiling? _____

_____

Are all income taxes paid in full?   ☐ Yes   ☐ No

Do any outstanding audits exist? ☐ Yes ☐ No

If yes, is it ☐ Federal and/or ☐ State For what tax year(s)? _____

Do you make quarterly estimated tax payments ☐ Yes ☐ No

If yes, does a CPA facilitate your quarterly tax payments? ☐ Yes ☐ No

CPA's name and contact information _____

_____

Personal Tax Returns (if someone else in household files separately)

Full Names(s) on most recent tax returns _____

_____

Indicate which filings are applicable to your household:

☐ Federal ☐ State

Name of Tax Return Preparer _____

Preparer's Contact Information _____

Do you prepare your own taxes online? ☐ Yes ☐ No

Note where online access, user name, password, and PIN information is located _____

_____

Location of copies of past tax returns _____

Do you keep an accumulation file for *Current Year's* tax information? ☐ Yes ☐ No

If yes, where is the file located? _____

Are all income tax filings current? ☐ Yes ☐ No

Have you recently had to refile a tax return? ☐ Yes ☐ No

If yes, is the refiling ☐ Federal and/or ☐ State List the tax year(s) _____

What is the reason for the refiling? _____

_____

Are all income taxes paid in full? ☐ Yes ☐ No

Do any outstanding audits exist?　☐ Yes　☐ No

If yes, is it　☐ Federal　and/or　☐ State　For what tax year(s)? _____

Do you make quarterly estimated tax payments　☐ Yes　☐ No

If yes, does a CPA facilitate your quarterly tax payments?　☐ Yes　☐ No

CPA's name and contact information _____

_____

Business Tax Returns

Business #1

Name of Business _____

Which filings are applicable to your business　☐ Federal　☐ State

Name of Tax Preparer _____

Preparer's Contact Information _____

Do you prepare your business taxes online?　☐ Yes　☐ No

If yes, list where website, username, password, and PIN information is located

_____

Location of copies of past tax returns _____

Indicate if you keep an accumulation file for *Current Year's* tax information and note the location of the file. _____

_____

Are all income tax filings current?　☐ Yes　☐ No

Have you recently had to refile a tax return?　☐ Yes　☐ No

If yes, is it　☐ Federal　and/or　☐ State　What is the tax year(s)? _____

What is the reason for the refiling? _____

Are all income taxes paid in full?　☐ Yes　☐ No

Do any outstanding audits exist?　☐ Yes　☐ No

If yes, is it　☐ Federal　and/or　☐ State　For what tax year(s)? _____

Do you make quarterly estimated tax payments? ☐ Yes ☐ No

If yes, does a CPA facilitate your quarterly tax payments? ☐ Yes ☐ No

CPA's Name and Contact Information _____

_____

Business #2

Name of Business _____

Which filings are applicable to your business ☐ Federal ☐ State

Name of Tax Preparer _____

Preparer's Contact Information _____

Do you prepare your business taxes online? ☐ Yes ☐ No

If yes, list where website, username, password, and PIN information is located

_____

Location of copies of past tax returns _____

Indicate if you keep an accumulation file for *Current Year's* tax information and note the location of the file. _____

_____

Are all income tax filings current? ☐ Yes ☐ No

Have you recently had to refile a tax return? ☐ Yes ☐ No

If yes, is it ☐ Federal and/or ☐ State   For what tax year(s)? _____

What is the reason for the refiling? _____

Are all income taxes paid in full? ☐ Yes ☐ No

Do any outstanding audits exist? ☐ Yes ☐ No

If yes, is it ☐ Federal and/or ☐ State   For what tax year(s)? _____

Do you make quarterly estimated tax payments? ☐ Yes ☐ No

If yes, does a CPA facilitate your quarterly tax payments? ☐ Yes ☐ No

CPA's Name and Contact Information _____

_____

Property Taxes

1. Property

Description _____

Address _____

City _____ State _____ Zip _____

Property in the Name of _____

Tax Due Date ___ / ___ / _____

2. Property

Description _____

Address _____

City _____ State _____ Zip _____

Property in the Name of _____

Tax Due Date ___ / ___ / _____

3. Property

Description _____

Address _____

City _____ State _____ Zip _____

Property in the Name of _____

Tax Due Date ___ / ___ / _____

4. Property

Description _____

Address _____

City _____ State _____ Zip _____

Property in the Name of _____

Tax Due Date ___ / ___ / _____

5. Property

Description _____

Address _____

City _____ State _____ Zip _____

Property in the Name of _____

Tax Due Date ___ / ___ / _____

6. Property

Description _____

Address _____

City _____ State _____ Zip _____

Property in the Name of _____

Tax Due Date ___ / ___ / _____

Changes and Additional Information (remember to date)

Changes and Additional Information (remember to date)

Changes and Additional Information (remember to date)

CHAPTER 9

Security Considerations

Up to this point, I have not suggested how you should keep the information you are documenting secure. Depending on your circumstances, you may intend to share your information with one or several individuals.

Should YOU decide to create an electronic version of the information you're documenting, I recommend you immediately password protect your electronic document. You need to share the fact that the document exists with the appropriate person(s). You can then:

✓ Tell them where the password can be found when needed

✓ Send them the password protected file and provide them with the password.

I caution you to **NOT** forward the file via an email and include the password in the same communication.

If the file is sent to others, consider providing the password verbally and ask them to keep it in a safe place. They should also disguise what the password is for, for obvious reasons.

Remember... if this is the way you chose to share your information make sure you send a revised file each time you update.

You will note that throughout this roadmap, I have provided space allowing you to note the information discussed and recommended for documentation.

If you should choose this option, be sure to inform the individuals you entrust that your TCB Folder and documentation exists. Then place this book in a home vault or a safe deposit box that your designee has access to, even after your death.

This will help eliminate the possibility of exposure to a wrong party.

Be sure to update your TCB Folder information when life changes occur.

If your children or close relatives live out of town, you may want to consider giving a close friend their contact information in case of an emergency.

In addition, you may want to share a key to your home (especially if you live alone) and certain medical information with someone that lives close to you. Everyone's personal situation dictates how and with whom they should share this information. I'm confident that after completing this task, you can better determine what information needs to be shared and with whom.

One other word of advice . . .

Never throw away anything in your trash with your name and address on it.

My husband used to give me a hard time about shredding everything from personalized envelopes, paid bills, to address labels on magazines. That is until a friend of his was a victim of *identity theft* with none other than the IRS!

Remember earlier I said the burden of proof is on the individual that has been caught up in identify theft?

Well, it took his friend years to get his business straight and now my husband is as diligent as I am about taking this precaution.

I am especially careful to tear off the label on catalogues where we have placed mail orders.

Did you know that once you place an order, a customer number becomes a part of future address labels? Often, the customer number ties back to a credit card you used to make the purchase. Imagine someone using this information fraudulently to order and ship to a different address, pretending the purpose of the order is for a gift!

Now that I've gotten your attention, let's look at some additional security considerations to include in your TCB document.

- **In-Home Safe** – location of the safe and key as well as a notation of the combination (or where it can be found).

- **Location of Spare Keys** – decide on and identify one location in your home to keep all extra keys for house, car, offsite storage, etc. and tag them accordingly.

- **Passwords for Computer** – note the main password as well as any separate password protected documents within your computer. It is critical that anytime you change a password that you note it immediately.

Note to self: _____

_____

_____

- **Home Alarm Code** – also note the security code/word that is required when the security company calls if an alarm is activated.

- **Security Company Name** – that provides your alarm service.

✓ **Do Not Call List** – while not always effective, I recommend individuals register their home, business and cell phone numbers on the *National Do Not Call List*. This can be accomplished on line at their website.

When receiving a solicitation call after registering, ask the caller if they checked the list before contacting you.

Legitimate solicitors should apologize and not call again. Scammers will ignore your question so hang up immediately. You can also block specific robocalls through this site as well.

✓ **Robocall Blocker** – there are apps you can purchase for your cell phones to block robocalls. Services can also be purchased to block calls to your home or business phones.

Never give solicitors information about anyone in your household or any personal facts. Also, be aware that no legitimate business will reach out to you via phone for information unless they are responding to a call *YOU* initiated, especially financial institutions, computer service providers, or the IRS. Scammers only want to coax you into turning over control of your computer or other information that could potentially harm you.

Recent scams have involved calling individuals and asking questions that require a "Yes" answer which they record to create your voice recognition. If you don't know the person calling . . . **HANG UP!**

Other Security Related Notes Relative to Your Situation.

Note to self: _____

_____

_____

_____

_____

_____

ROADMAP

Security Considerations Checklist

Location of Home Safe _____

Location of Key/Combination _____

Location of Spare Keys for Home, Car, Storage, etc. _____

_____

_____

Note: I recommend all keys be kept in a central location and tagged for identification purposes.

Location of password information for both computer and password protected documents

_____

Note: I recommend keeping password information in a secure place.

Home Alarm Code _____

Alarm code password for a false alarm _____

Home Security Provided by _____

Contact Information _____

List any social media accounts (Facebook, Instagram, Twitter, LinkedIn, Snapchat, Google or any other media account launched in the future) that you have set up along with the corresponding User Name and Password. _____

_____

_____

Other Security Related Notes _____

_____

_____

_____

Changes and Additional Information (remember to date)

Changes and Additional Information (remember to date)

Changes and Additional Information (remember to date)

CHAPTER 10
Estate Planning

Spending forty plus years in banking taught me that one of the most difficult tasks we face *is addressing our Estate Planning*. Yet a lack of addressing such plans can sometimes create the greatest and most costly challenges for our loved ones.

No one likes to think about the day we may not be able to take care of ourselves or will no longer exist on earth. We need to face the fact that the latter is inevitable.

I have also witnessed sincere relief and peace once individuals addressed this task. It is never too early to create a will and I used to advise my clients,

---

"Once you start working, marry, accumulating assets . . . and especially when you have children, you need a WILL."

Obviously the older you get and the more complex your life and/or holdings become, the more you will need to consider if your original will provisions are still adequate. Family dynamics differ from one family to another. You will need to decide who you trust to name as the executor of your estate.

If you choose someone other than an attorney or corporate entity, I highly recommend you have conversations with the individual(s) to not only make sure they are comfortable being named executor but also to give them the opportunity to ask questions and truly understand your intentions.

Also consider the difficulty of naming multiple people to perform this duty at the time of your death, especially if they live in different states. Discuss this issue with the attorney that assists you in creating your will. If appropriate, I also recommend having a conversation with all family members ahead of time concerning your wishes. This eliminates your designated executor from dealing with questions they may not be able to answer.

Below is a list of suggested information necessary for someone to take care of your affairs if you become incapacitated or when the time comes for guidance on your final wishes.

- 🖉 **Estate Attorney's Name and Contact Information.**

- 🖉 **Copy of the Will** – date of your most recent will and the location of the document.

🖋 **Power of Attorney** – indicate if you have created a general power of attorney (POA) for someone to act on your behalf. Note that most banks/investment firms prefer their own POA for giving authority to someone to sign on your accounts.

NOTE: Adding someone to an account may be construed as giving them equal ownership, where a POA does not give ownership and is null and void at your death.

🖋 **Bank POA** – if you HAVE granted a specific power of attorney for bank/investment accounts, list them all separately and indicate the individual that you've assigned this authority.

🖋 **Bequests Outside of Your Will** – you may have family heirlooms, antiques, jewelry, art and other things that you may want to bequest to others that aren't noted in your will. Be sure to note such items and give your executor power to distribute according to your wishes. Typically, your will may state that you may have left separate instructions for the distribution of personal items.

When designating very valuable personal items make sure the bequest is noted in the will.

Note to self: _____

_____

_____

_____

_____

_____

📁 **Family Pictures or Movies** – consider dividing up family photos/movies that have been collected throughout the years and placing them in individual keepsake boxes. Write your children/grandchildren/relative's names on each box based on how you want them distributed later. In the meantime, you can still pull them out and view them anytime you wish.

🖋 **Family Heirlooms** – consider tagging family heirlooms or keepsakes that you wish to pass down to relatives, along with details of their origin. They will truly appreciate having this information.

Note to self: _____

_____

_____

_____

_____

_____

📁 **Life Insurance Policies** – already noted in **Chapter 7: Insurance**.

📁 **Certificates of Birth, Marriage, and Divorce** – strongly consider placing copies of these certificates in your **TCB Folder**. In addition, if you have a spouse or child that predeceased you, consider placing copies of their death certificates as well. All such information may help aid the executor of your estate.

📁 **Military Records** – if applicable place them in your **TCB Folder**.

📁 **Trust Documents** – often individuals make a decision to leave their estate in a trust for their beneficiaries vs. leaving assets outright. Trusts can be created during your lifetime or by provisions contained in your will. You and your attorney can discuss in detail your wishes for how the assets are to be disbursed overtime and if the trust is to last over multiple generations or terminated at a certain age of the beneficiaries.

You will also need to name a trustee and that may be either an individual (relative, friend or attorney) or corporate trustee such as a bank or trust company.

Choose carefully as the trustee will need to be knowledgeable and strong enough to not only manage the assets placed in the trust but to adhere to your original intent and follow the terms of the trust. Often beneficiaries try to sway individuals (especially family members) to grant more flexibility than provided for in the trust. If a trust has been established, note where a copy of the trust can be found and the name and contact information of the trustee. If the trust was created during your lifetime, the trustee should have the *original* trust instrument. If it is created in your will, it will not be in existence until your death.

- **Executor of Another Individual's Will** – document if you are named as the executor of someone else's will, indicating their name and contact information. Obviously, this will need to be addressed if you are no longer able to serve in this role due to incapacitation or death.

- **Burial Arrangements** – information on any existing arrangements, burial plots or burial vaults. Again, make sure a trusted family member or friend knows exactly where these are located along with evidence of ownership.

- **Funeral and Burial Requests** – include the name of the funeral home of preference. Consider pre-arrangements including writing your own obituary.

Note to self: _____

_____

_____

_____

_____

_____

- **Family Tree** – if you have researched your ancestry and have information, this information is good to include in your **TCB Folder**.

Other Documentation to Include:

_____

_____

_____

_____

_____

_____

I have always said that inherited wealth was easier to spend than money you worked hard to earn! That being said, think seriously about the individuals that will inherit from you and whether they are financially responsible and/or are easily influenced by a spouse or other family members.

Unfortunately, any inheritance may put them in awkward situations someday. However, carefully thought out estate planning on your part may help alleviate some of that.

I recall a situation where a client's child was never really motivated to become self-supporting until they learned their parents were leaving their estate in trusts (vs. outright inheritance) to all the surviving children. The trusts were set up to distribute an amount, on an annual basis, equal to what each particular child *earned annually* on their own.

Needless to say, the unmotivated child had second thoughts about their future and turned their life around. Every family's situation is different therefore it is important to plan according to what is best for yours.

And don't forget about the many worthwhile organizations that serve the needs of others, including your church. Consider establishing an endowment or making charitable bequests through your will, which will make a huge difference in the lives of others someday.

ROADMAP

Estate Planning

Will and Estate Planning

1. Full Legal Name _____

Do you have a Will? ☐ Yes ☐ No   Do you have an estate plan? ☐ Yes ☐ No

Name of Will or Estate Plan Attorney _____

_____

_____

Contact Information _____

_____

Date of Will ___ / ___ / _____   Date of Estate Plan ___ / ___ / _____

Designated Executor(s) and Contact Information _____

_____

Copy of Will/Estate Plan Location _____

_____

Trust has been created ☐ Yes ☐ No

Date of Trust ___ / ___ / _____

Designated Trustee(s) and Contact Information _____

_____

Copy of Trust Document Location _____

_____

Power of Attorney Exists ☐ Yes ☐ No *If yes,* a copy is located _____

Note if a separate Power of Attorney exists for any of your bank/investment accounts. **Most banks will not accept a general POA.** List any accounts below along with the individual that you have assigned this authority.

_____

_____

_____

Bequests outside of your will. I recommend creating a list on a separate document and have it notarized and file it with your will.

Note: Items of significant monetary value should be NOTED in your will.

Are you an executor of another individual's will? ☐ Yes ☐ No

If yes, list their name and your relationship to the individual _____

_____

Are you the trustee of another individual's Trust? ☐ Yes ☐ No

If yes, list their name and your relationship to the individual _____

_____

Funeral and Burial Arrangement

☐ Organ Donor   ☐ Anatomical (body) Donor

Funeral Home of Preference _____

Location _____

Pre-arrangements have been made ☐ Yes ☐ No

I prefer ☐ Embalmment ☐ Cremation

Gravesite Preference and Location _____

Gravesite Already Exists ☐ Yes ☐ No

Tombstone Established ☐ Yes ☐ No

Existing Columbarium ☐ Yes ☐ No

If yes, Location and Niche # _____

I have a Prewritten Obituary ☐ Yes ☐ No

If yes, indicate where it is located _____

List contact information of people other than family members and locals that you would like to be notified of your passing. Consider making a list and placing it in your **TCB Folder.** Note here if that has been done ☐

Family Tree

Note here any existence of ancestry research and/or the documentation of your family tree. Indicate where the information can be found. Include username and password to any research website you used.

_____

_____

_____

_____

Other Notes/Documentation Concerning Your Estate or Wishes

_____

_____

_____

_____

_____

_____

_____

2. Full Legal Name (for a separate individual's documentation i.e. spouse)

_____

Do you have a Will? ☐ Yes ☐ No   Do you have an estate plan? ☐ Yes ☐ No

Name of Will or Estate Plan Attorney _____

_____

_____

Contact Information _____

_____

Date of Will ___ / ___ / _____   Date of Estate Plan ___ / ___ / _____

Designated Executor(s) and Contact Information _____

_____

Copy of Will/Estate Plan Location _____

_____

Trust has been created ☐ Yes ☐ No

Date of Trust ___ / ___ / _____

Designated Trustee(s) and Contact Information _____

_____

Copy of Trust Document Location _____

_____

Power of Attorney Exists ☐ Yes ☐ No _If yes,_ a copy is located _____

_____

Note if a separate Power of Attorney exists for any of your bank/investment accounts. **Most banks will not accept a general POA**. List any accounts below along with the individual that you have assigned this authority.

_____

_____

_____

Bequests outside of your will. I recommend creating a list on a separate document and have it notarized and file it with your will.

Note: Items of significant monetary value should be NOTED in your will.

Are you an executor of another individual's will? ☐ Yes ☐ No

If yes, list their name and your relationship to the individual _____

_____

Are you the trustee of another individual's Trust? ☐ Yes ☐ No

If yes, list their name and your relationship to the individual _____

_____

Funeral and Burial Arrangement

☐ Organ Donor   ☐ Anatomical (body) Donor

Funeral Home of Preference _____

Location _____

Pre-arrangements have been made ☐ Yes ☐ No

I prefer ☐ Embalmment   ☐ Cremation

Gravesite Preference and Location _____

Gravesite Already Exists ☐ Yes ☐ No

Tombstone Established ☐ Yes ☐ No

Existing Columbarium ☐ Yes ☐ No

If yes, Location and Niche # _____

I have a Prewritten Obituary ☐ Yes ☐ No

If yes, indicate where it is located _____

List contact information of people other than family members and locals that you would like to be notified of your passing. Consider making a list and placing it in your **TCB Folder.** Note here if that has been done ☐

Family Tree

Note here any existence of ancestry research and/or the documentation of your family tree. Indicate where the information can be found. Include username and password to any research website you used.

_____

_____

_____

_____

Other Notes/Documentation Concerning Your Estate or Wishes

_____

_____

_____

_____

_____

_____

_____

_____

Changes and Additional Information (remember to date)

Changes and Additional Information (remember to date)

CHAPTER 11

Miscellaneous Things to Address in Handling My Estate

Some of what I'll share with you here has been mentioned in previous chapters. However, this is an additional reminder of things that will need cancelling or addressing when handling your estate.

Consider making a copy of the checklist at the **end of this chapter, highlighting** the items that pertain to your circumstances, and including them in your **TCB Folder.** Realize that everything on this list might not be relative to you OR there may be instructions you need to add.

Tailor the checklist to your personal situation.

- 📁 **Social Security Administration** – should be notified if monthly benefits are being received in the name of the deceased. In most cases, funeral homes will contact SSA but be sure to confirm. In many cases a surviving spouse would qualify/benefit from the transfer or substitution of SS benefits once received by the deceased. This would be another good reason to contact the Social Security Administration directly.

- 📁 **Disability Benefits** – the payor of the benefits should be notified to either facilitate the transfer of benefits to the surviving spouse or stop the monthly payment depending on the circumstances.

- 📁 **Pension Benefits** – should be stopped or transferred to a spouse if that provision exists. A separate beneficiary designation form should have already been completed (and/or updated). Original should be with the payor of the benefits but consider putting a copy in your **TCB Folder.**

- 📁 **Bank Drafts/Automatic Deposits** – any automatic bank drafts related to services used by the deceased (only) should be canceled upon death.

The same goes for automatic deposits for benefits that cease at one's death. Drafts or deposits that benefit both the deceased and a remaining joint owner can continue until the joint account is eventually closed.

📁 **Credit Cards** – in the name of the deceased should be cancelled as soon as possible. The executor should list any outstanding balance as a liability of the estate.

📁 **Bank Accounts** – Note that accounts in the sole name of a deceased will eventually need to be closed but can no longer be accessed with a power of attorney.

As mentioned in an earlier chapter, POAs are null and void at the death of the grantor. Also, remember to check with your bank concerning their policy on freezing joint accounts when one owner dies. As soon as possible I recommend that a new account be opened for the surviving spouse/partner to operate from.

📁 **Estate Checking Account** – In almost all situations, it will be necessary to open an estate checking account.

This is in order to process the collection of proceeds payable to the estate, including sale of assets; reimbursement from insurance claims (other than life insurance which has a named beneficiary) and any income from other sources owned by or payable to the estate. The account will need to remain open until the estate is completely settled.

Note that a new Tax ID number will be required as the social security number of the deceased is no longer appropriate (as the estate is a different entity). Some banks can obtain the needed Tax ID number for you as part of the account opening process. An original death certificate will be needed in order to obtain the new Tax ID number.

📁 **Cell Phone** – Cancel service contract as soon as possible, especially if the cost is automatically charged to an account on a monthly basis. Home phone service may need to be canceled as well, depending on the circumstances, such as someone continuing to live in the home.

📁 **Memberships** – cancel any memberships applicable as identified in the TCB document.

📁 **Computer, Cable, Alarm Services** – if applicable, cancel any services as stipulated in the TCB document.

📁 **Social Media Accounts** – cancel accounts that the deceased may have established on Facebook, Instagram, Tweeter or Snap Chat. Facebook accounts specifically contain pictures and other personal information and are often targeted by scammers.

📁 **Disclosure of Death via the Phone** – use caution in disclosing the death of a loved one to an unknown caller over the phone, especially if the deceased is your spouse/partner. Ask the caller to identify themselves and simply say the party they are trying to reach is not available.

📁 **Insurance** – As the designated individual, notify all life, health and long-term care insurance providers of your loved one's death so that billing will stop. At the time of notification, you or the estate executor should request the necessary forms to file claims for stated benefits. In the case of health or long-term care coverage, appropriate forms would be needed to submit claims for any outstanding service provider bills.

Typically, the forms would indicate instructions for other documentation needed to complete the claim. But note, each entity notified will require an **original** death certificate, so depending on the complexity of the estate, multiple copies should be requested and are provided by the funeral home for a small fee per document.

📁 **Asset Appraisals** – a very important part of administering an estate is to have assets appraised, especially if they are to be sold.

Real estate, used vehicles, art, jewelry, antiques, and collections of any sort could all be mistakenly sold for less than their actual value.

📁 **Death Certificates** – additional certificates can be obtained through the state's office of vital records if needed.

Remember, you will *need an original vs. a photo copy* for each insurance company, bank or investment company, retirement plan, etc. where proof of death will be needed in order to proceed with settling any monies due or sale of assets. As noted, the funeral home will provide as many copies as needed for a nominal fee.

📁 **Mail** – consider whether it is necessary to have mail forwarded to another address.

📁 **Driving License and Passports** – as mentioned prior, these should be cancelled to prevent potential identity theft.

As technology improves, this may not be necessary someday but better to be safe than sorry.

✎ **Other Considerations** – unique to your personal circumstances.

Note to self: _____

_____

_____

_____

_____

Since you are reading this in preparation for documenting your own affairs, this final issue would not necessarily apply to you. But perhaps you are in the midst of helping settle someone else's affairs where there were NO complete records or instructions left behind.

The issue concerns "unclaimed" or "escheated" property. Property that at one time belonged to the now deceased, in many cases a person without an heir. After a substantial period of time of no contact from the rightful owner or their representative, the unclaimed property is transferred to the state where the deceased was domiciled.

It remains property of the state until legally claimed by the owner or one of their heirs. Such assets are listed on each state's individual website categorized as either Unclaimed Property or Escheated Property. Most unclaimed property can be identified by searching the person's name.

Examples of such assets might be real estate, stocks and bonds, bank accounts, mineral rights, etc. Forms for claiming these assets are typically available on the same website. Consult an attorney if you should need further instructions.

ROADMAP

Checklist of Miscellaneous Things to Address in Handling My Estate

Consider sharing this checklist with the one that will handle your affairs after your passing. These will need to be addressed in addition to your will and estate plan. This will aid them in Taking Care of Business.

☐ **Social Security** must be notified. While most funeral homes do this as part of their process, confirm that this was done. In many cases, a surviving spouse would qualify/benefit from the transfer of benefits to them, another reason to contact Social Security Administration.

☐ **Disability Benefits** payor should be notified. A surviving spouse may qualify to receive full or partial benefits.

☐ **Pension Benefits** payor should be notified. A surviving spouse may qualify to receive full or partial benefits. A copy of the beneficiary designation form should be placed in a **TCB Folder.**

☐ **Cancelation of Bank Drafts, Automatic Deposits, etc.** that were payable to the deceased or for the benefit of the deceased and are no longer applicable.

☐ **Note that a Power of Attorney is null and void at time of death.** All accounts in the deceased separate name and any joint accounts will need to be closed once estate is settled. As soon as possible, a new account should be opened for the surviving spouse/partner to operate from.

☐ **Cancelation of Credit Cards** in the name of the deceased.

☐ **Open an Estate Checking Account** – this may be necessary for distribution of assets (without a named beneficiary) or for the payment of outstanding liabilities before non-designated assets are distributed. Note that a new tax ID number will be required as the social security number of the deceased cannot be used.

☐ **Cancel Cell Phone Service** or at a minimum remove the deceased's phone number from the account.

☐ **Cancel Memberships** related to the deceased's exclusive usage.

☐ **Cancel Any Home/Equipment Service Providers** if the deceased lived alone and services are no longer needed by other residents.

☐ **Cancel Social Media Accounts** in the name of the deceased.

☐ **Notify All Insurance Providers** and request necessary forms to complete outstanding medical care claims and/or those necessary to process receipt of beneficiary payouts.

☐ **Original Death Certificates** – Multiple copies should be requested as each provider notified or claim requested will require an original copy. In most cases, the funeral home will provide these for a nominal fee per original.

☐ **Appraise Assets** – Important step before selling or disbursing assets (especially when trying to equalize the value of assets that are distributed to beneficiaries).

☐ **Cancel Driver's License and Passport** in order to help prevent identify theft.

☐ **Mail** – decide if it needs to be forwarded to another address.

List Additional Considerations that are unique to the deceased individual's personal circumstances.

_____

_____

_____

_____

_____

_____

Changes and Additional Information (remember to date)

Changes and Additional Information (remember to date)

CONCLUSION

I hope that you have found the information in this roadmap useful. More importantly, I hope that you have made the decision to document the necessary information that will assist your family members someday. You will feel tremendous relief when your project is done . . . and so will they.

I want to leave you with one more personal story that relates to sharing information with a loved one. My family and I were blessed with a loving stepfather that passed away years before our Mother. While we were all grown by the time he and Mother married, he always welcomed us into their home and treated us like his own, especially the grandchildren.

After his funeral, our Mother presented us with sealed envelopes addressed to us individually, personal letters that he had handwritten before he died. It was his final message to us, expressing his love and encouraging us to continue growing in our careers, family, and faith. I still pull my letter out and read it occasionally, to lift my spirits.

You might consider a similar final message to those closest to you. Just a thought . . .

Phyllis W. McLaurin is a retired Financial Advisor/Market Manager who spent 42 years in banking. She began her career at Wachovia Bank and Trust in North Carolina as one of their first female management trainees. In 2013, she retired as Managing Director of Private Banking from JPMorgan Chase Bank in Baton Rouge, Louisiana.

The majority of her career was spent working with professionals, executives, and clients with varying financial needs. While she thrived at building, working, and managing a team, her first love was working with individual clients, helping them address and manage their assets and financial future.

She states that one of her greatest accomplishments was moving to Baton Rouge in 1977 and developing new clients, one at a time. Her philosophy of listening to individuals and providing the best service possible allowed her to grow a client base beyond her own imagination.

In addition to her full-time job as a banker, wife, and mother, she found time to get involved in the community. Phyllis has served on numerous professional and non-profit boards over the years. In addition, she is heavily involved with VIPs (Volunteers in Public Schools) and tutor's young students in reading. Phyllis has also spent time helping friends settle the affairs of their family members. She has also conducted many sessions educating individuals on preparing their loved ones to take care of them someday.

Phyllis graduated from Hardbarger's Business College in Raleigh, NC and the Graduate School of Banking at Louisiana State University. She has been married to Lee McLaurin since 1976 and has a son, two stepdaughters and nine grandchildren.

www.ingramcontent.com/pod-product-compliance
Lightning Source LLC
Chambersburg PA
CBHW081814200326
41597CB00023B/4243